THE OCHRE HAND

A Life Lived

DON ERDEK

Simon Publishing LLC

Simon Publishing LLC

Naples, Florida

Cover Design by Joe Eckstein, Image Studios www.ArtsImagine.com

Cover Images: IStock.com/Goldfinsh4ever, IStock.com/sapfirr

Library of Congress Control Number: 2020912778

ISBN: 978-0-578-23587-5

First Edition

PREFACE

An Ochre Handprints have been found on ancient rocks and on the walls of ancient caves worldwide.

They aren't regarded as works of art but nor should they be regarded as meaningless ancient exercises.

These ubiquitous drawings have a deeper meaning and I believe them to be a declaration of life by an individual.

A long-ago human being recognized his solitary existence and it was his way of profoundly declaring "I lived", "I existed ""This is my proof."

This truism is common to every human whoever walked this earth.

A unique existence within one body, one mind.

A universality each of us possesses.

The *Ochre Hand* is written to capture snippets of one life in a series of poems, stories, and essays compiled over several decades.

It is the author's own ochre handprint set in print.

It is meant to entertain because life is a joy; to evoke discussion because we all differ in thought, and to show the commonality in all of us.

An individual's existence in one's own time and world space.

≈

MAIN DIVISIONS

TIME..6

AGED..43

LIGHT..78

STORIES..116

ESSAYS..213

ABOUT THE AUTHOR........................322

≈

TIME

THE STROLL 8
INTROSPECTION - THE KEY 9
WELL SAID AND SAD 12
DARE TO SEEK ALONE TIME 13
THE DASH 15
THE GIFT 16
FRIENDSHIP 18
REALITY 19
LISTEN TO ME LISA 20
RITE OF PASSAGE 22
A MOMENT IN TIME 24
THE RIGHT NOW 26
TIME PASSAGES 29
MEDITATION 30
CLARION CALL 31
EXISTENCE 32
TIME AND FATE 33
PAUSE 34
GONE 35
WATCH WORDS TO AN OLD FRIEND 36
LIFE 37
SEARCH 38
SOLILOQUY OF ESCAPE 39
TURN AROUND 39
RESOLUTIONS 39

≈

TIME

Time marches on.

It is the most fundamental of life's yardsticks.

Rome today is different from that of Caesar's time.

Each life today realizes it had a genesis, a birth.

All life events are locked into a specific time.

All stories or happenings move along a timeline.

Each life is like a personal string of multi-colored pearls.

Some glorious white, others dark and shadowy.

Some rosy, some pale, each set upon a string of time.

No order to the color or shape.

A glorious one next to one misshapen and pale.

made for me to enjoy.

With the wind on my face I can feel the invisible air.

My eyes see only the empty transparency of Earth's atmosphere.

I cannot see those floating atoms yet I can feel them when they move as a blowing wind.

They are there no doubt, whether I see them or not.

There seems to be so many of nature's mysteries like that.

Feel hot and cold but not see it.

Smell an aroma but not feel or see it.

Hear a sound but neither see, feel, nor smell it.

Leaves one to wonder what things are beyond our five senses.

Our sensory powers limited to the essential.

No daily need for the extraordinary.

Or might I not have this quite right?

Might it be humans are limited for reasons undetermined?

Humans, who from elsewhere or nowhere, were formed in this place.

Where the sense of air about and the sand below developed only to fill a need.

I take for granted that Earth has always been here.

THE STROLL

An early morning stroll planting staccato footprints on a fresh wash of sugar white sands at Barefoot Beach.

Looking faraway across Bonita Bay.

The horizon but a silver sliver splitting the wideness of the sky from the calm nakedness of cobalt- blue water.

The start of another wonderful day of my life.

Where the solitary and emptiness of time taps into primordial yearnings.

The search to find one's self and one's place in the universe.

The sun rising at my back.

The sky bluing above my head.

The beach sand glistening beneath my feet.

The sea calm and serene capturing my gaze.

A bit of heaven,

A day in paradise,

All for me.

How wonderful a gift of life from Earth,

the Sun,

the infinite Cosmos,

Made for me with blue in the sky and water for a sea.

Breathe the air, smell it's freshness, select the oxygen to make my blood sound.

Frolic in the waters merely for fun.

My feet amble across the sand's of nature's wonders.

My mind strolling along in ignorant ecstasy that it all be for me.

≈

INTROSPECTION - THE KEY

In each of us there is something special.

At the creation of the universe, there was a special something.

It is what religions seek to find.

A belief in something greater, something special.

Something more than the universe itself.

Seeking that something special must be done one lifetime at a time.

Not words enough to explain not thought enough to expend.

Not understanding enough for one with but a frail yet almighty existence.

The individual realizes his true nature only by bringing self into harmony with the universal purpose.

Above all know thyself, know how thou does think.

The key to real freedom is introspection.

Sense perception and reason can give us knowledge of the world of physical things.

However the higher realm of the spiritual is of such difficulty that only a few accede.

If you don't know yourself, if you don't rely on your own judgments, you've wasted a lifetime.

Take time to think.

Everyone should take time to think - so few do.

Time to think is quiet time - time alone.

Not many allow themselves this privilege - this passage to true freedom.

A freedom to trust oneself and one's own judgments.

To avoid being a clone of someone else or a composite of many.

How does one find oneself if not alone - by oneself?

When others are around it is too easy to become a part of the group rather than an entity of self.

Others seldom let you be - simply you.

Truth is if you don't give yourself time to think you will be unable to find yourself.

Thinking is something you can neither buy nor sell.

So do you think or do you merely repeat what you heard someone else say?

Do you think or merely regurgitate what you heard on the evening news?

Are your morals and ethics defined lock, stock and barrel by some politician, pundit, priest, religious leader with little of your own critique?

Is the media and their monomaniacal, self-serving talking heads your enlightenment - your source for knowledge and truths?

That's not thinking - that's listening!

How many never move beyond being told how to live as well as what, when, and how to think?

Do many take more than an instant to answer a question and not much more to decide pro-choice or not?

Or to enter some silly, inane debate about whether or not women should be allowed in combat.

As if war is not the true issue for mankind's resolution.

Is deep thought avoided as a waste of time?

Is all opinion shunted to cyberspace?

And is cyberspace mostly a forward and seldom a new?

So let me provide you a first guide.

Take more time for your conscience, your soul, to provide direction.

Linger there a little longer and take time to recall those memories and knowledge you stored for future time.

Well, the future is in the here and now, whether you know it or not, or even like it or not.

Take time enough to analyze and judge.

That in it may be wisdom enough.

Don Erdek

WELL SAID AND SAD

Time is like a river.

You cannot touch the water twice.

The flow will never pass again.

Let's toss this around and expand.

A river is like time; you see not the same water.

Light is like time; the picture you see moves with light speed.

The flow that has passed will never pass again.

On Earth it is water that indicates change.

In the big scheme of things it is light upon which we float.

The moment before is now an age gone.

To be aware.

To be curious.

It is change which becomes life.

Life is ever in change.

It is indeed the evolution we live.

In spite of its light speed the Universe changes slowly; whereas humanity demands rapid change.

We and our actions to be mundane and uncivil are outpacing our intelligence to be thoughtful and civil.

Our search for change, our demands for change, are not in pace with our slowly evolving brain.

The brain is slow yet the mind speeds ahead making changes without markers, without a destiny in sight.

Self-destruction will result, yet water and time and the big scheme of things will continue to flow.

≈

DARE TO SEEK ALONE TIME

One who likes to be alone has found the ability to focus for long periods.

A unique skill of the introvert.

A propensity for balanced and critical thinking.

Not caring to change anyone else.

Yet when one does speak have that knack for quietly empowering others.

That is if others chose to listen.

Within introspective time there is that possibility to better find the truth about the most important things.

To linger on those amazing things mankind has made.

To be saddened by the horrors that the human race has perpetuated.

To marvel about the tiny planet Earth that is home.

Begin to realize Earth is not flat.

Realizing it was formed in a far out, unassuming location in the Milky Way galaxy.

We can't claim choice nor Eden-central location.

How big the Universe; how small and insignificant are we.

How magnificent is that which we call life.

How we, the top of the chain, are aware and curious of it all.

Introspection leads to examining creativity.

To ponder on desires,

love and treachery,

sorrow and joy,

foolishness and serenity,

hope and fear,

face death alone,

desire law and justice.

Ah! Law and Justice!

Those Senators the last three weeks.

Endless talk about the ills but not about the cure.

Talk from many mouths going past the many ears.

All those words sonically transmitted.

Un-attentive ear drums; bypassing any brain openings.

There was no engagement.
No introspection.
Posture and politics held sway.
Only embarrassment to an intelligent race.

≈

THE DASH

Lingering in a cemetery.
Drawn to the chiseled engravings.
Seeking peace like the souls entombed.
Future has departed this lonely place.

Cold and rigid these gray monuments.
Lacking the soft warmth of life's loves,
the heat in the many passions,
the change from year to year.

Upon each gravestone.
The day of birth.
The date of death.
Tucked between the two the dash.

The chiseled dash meaningless.

Unfair to romance and desires.

Potential and lust hammered into discarded chips and dust.

An entire life shrunk into a merest mark.

A symbol lacking bravado.

Ignoring life's joys and sorrows.

Cavalier to dismiss all essence.

So much omitted, the wind, the rain, the weather.

The hopes, the pains, the spills, the thrills.

The giggles, the laughs.

The children bred, a friend betrayed.

The efforts, the failures.

The things discovered, the knowledge gained.

A dash so vacant of meaning.

Unintentionally pronouncing the race is over.

THE GIFT

To be human and to be here for most any length of time is as rich a gift as one can receive.

To know, to be aware...Oh! What an added gift that is.

So rich is the knowledge that life continues with each new sunrise.

So hard to contemplate, so hard to contend that this entity does decay.

Possibly debarking on to a Stygian shore.

Hoping instead for a coup de grace with setting in Elysium.

None to be spared.

None get out alive.

The clock stops ticking for all eventually.

No amount of sorrow or tears to cause a return.

A return to what?

When more time is never enough.

Death's winged chariot draws ever near.

A bomb of death it carries.

A missile so lethal as to reduce a self to dust.

Each aging year multiplies the fear.

There is no announcement on the timing.

No notice when it arrives.

It spreads its cold terror even while a life is lived.

Let us not despair, instead we must be up and doing.

To each his own ever pursuing.

The light behind the eyes must set the course.

The will to live guides the path.

Each individual draws its own breath.

Each heart pumps alone.

≈

FRIENDSHIP

This may sound harsh, it is not meant to be.

Honesty is all there is.

If you're looking for a friend…I'm it.

If you're looking for some fun...I'm up for that.

If you're expecting someone to understand you or stroke your ego...forget me.

Don't get in the way of my freedom and independence and I won't trample yours.

I want no ties, no downtime, and no long-term commitments.

I'm open to new friendships or to go back to good old ones.

Where I am now is where I want to be...free.

I am now truly happy doing things that are good for me.

I have found some joy in life and don't want anyone to steal it from me.

The past is no longer important.

The future is yet to be.

The only time that truly matters is "NOW"

≈

REALITY

In the timeless universe there spins a globe.

On its crust sit a tiny animal called man.

Dealing not with the vastness.

Concentrating on the small.

Man is harnessed to the thin veneer of planet Earth.

So plain to see, so small and limited is he.

So insignificant is the expanse of his domain.

So foolish the vision it all be made for him.

How limited his reach to the vastness he knows to be way beyond.

Created over the eons as the scattering from supernova.

Life became an exceptional association of carbon and minerals and water.

Death a return to non-biological elemental scattering.

However there-in lies the magnificence of man ... knowing.

He is aware of it all.

He knows he has been created and evolved on this planet.

His body, his brain may be made from dirt, air and water but his mind senses it all..

Conscious of time and space all the way back from here to there where the micro-static remains.

All this time, all this space, all that matters has evolved.

The universe is evolving still.

Sometimes fast, other times slow, but always steady of purpose.

It is that reality which must be addressed.

To that reality must be the focus.

Dust, dirt, ash, air, water, darkness...the boundaries on both sides of brilliance.

≈

LISTEN TO ME LISA

There is a fast speed, slow speed and then old speed.

Old speed is a just above idle speed.

A pace just right to get it done exactly in time for someone else to do it.

The time when need-to becomes ought-to.

When time is clocked by no clock other than a beating heart.

A heart which pauses now and then to check if the pulse is still there.

Where nimble fingers are not needed only because they no longer exist.

Where sharp as a tack resides only in a tack since the mind once sharp has become blunted and flat.

Where the head must be correctly angled for the eyes to focus.

In any event the lumens of light are never enough.

Where fingers are too stiff and thumbs too many.

Where the help from others only highlight lack of agility and onset of senility.

Where luminous and radiant are now lummox and dim.

So dear Lisa listen to me.

Why bother me, why care?

I now act funny and think slow.

Being old and worn-out is so obvious.

Now I hope you don't take wrong what I'm about to say.

Leave me alone is the best way.

≈

Don Erdek

RITE OF PASSAGE

Brief the years of puberty and adolescence.

When immaturity causes turmoil.

No need to distinguish sense from nonsense.

In high school no attention paid to grammar or sentence structure.

Inattentive to teachers urging and scolding.

No time allowed for syntax, linguistics, or speaking truths.

Days of youth spent in wild pursuit of fun and games.

Laughs and giggles, rakish talk, filled most moments of a young boy's time.

Vast the mountain of boyish dreams chock full of prankish schemes.

Most of the problem was simply youth.

Unprepared to address anything that did not excite.

An immature lad with hormones churning cares not about a dangling participle.

Especially when the participle seldom dangles.

Between classes having to walk with notebook in front.

Below the belt to conceal an uncontrollable protrusion.

Thinking of a young lass willing to split an infinitive.

Never a wrestle between conscience and concentration.

When neither occupy any mental location.

All areas in a lad's psychic and attention subsumed by a big set or pretty ass and if lucky, both.

Ignoring a lass's dreams packed full of prince charming, a white castle and happiness ever after.

If a sentence was to run on, that was fine by any standard.

Asked about a gerund or the genitive the reply would be "I never touched her".

Never want to correct or covert anyone else's grammar.

At least never in public, always in private.

A book with no pictures beyond the ability.

If not dumb-down, it was pure futility.

Never understood why book reports of comics were unacceptable.

There never was time given to clear thinking.

Learning to decide right from wrong coming from the seat of the pants.

Or better yet, by way of some girl's panties.

Never did allow a learning process to interfere with a good beer.

Both mind and character took a back seat to what could be done in a backseat.

Hoping that young lass would cast logic and caution aside and agree to splitting hairs.

Too quickly, in too soon time, did changes come.

Soon a family and mouths to feed.

From dawn to dusk, from hand to mouth, no time for the intellect.

No time for Spinoza, Plato, Kant, Locke, Saul of Tarsus, or for that matter the Constitution.

Spare time and more consumed with seeking a living solution.

Too busy taking care of business.

Doing things that come easy and not those that don't.

Doing what comes natural with no time for religion or precision.

Those were the years ago when there was no need for learning or smarts.

Why take time to read when you believe you are clever enough.

≈

A MOMENT IN TIME

The right now is always the right time.

Moments of life appreciated.

The sense of breath, the view of one's hand, the novel lines of the palm.

Accepting when old the right now is no different than of youth.

Past steps of life, one moment at a time, each replaces the one before.

Ever in lock step with the advancing years.

Each moment becomes our life to remember, unique to self.

The accumulation is life past.

The speculation is moments yet to be.

Each moment adds richness to life with instances of memory.

Sentiments grow strong grower.

Sentiments to define life itself, retaining those of value.

As yesteryear fades, experience lingers.

Experience of past moments in time.

Youthful moments of speculation start to dim, often but a flicker.

Ever the most precious moment is the one right now.

It can open the mind to a new thought or become a different slant on an old one.

It is the joy of being alive.

It can be as effortless as noticing the glistening of frost on the morning grass.

Capturing a sunset of changing hue.

Simple as realizing now is the time to define a new moment.

Don Erdek

THE RIGHT NOW

The right now is always right now.

How alarming is it to realize that when old the right now is no different than the right now of one's youth.

Those moments in time when you are aware of being alive, you can sense yourself breathe, or can view a hand and explore the lines in your palm.

As we step through life, a moment at a time, each moment replaces the one before.

They are those moments of time which is ever in lock-step with the advancing years.

These moments in time become our life to remember - unique to each of us.

The accumulation of which is our life past.

The speculation of which becomes our life to be.

The older we get the richer our life becomes with moments of memory.

The older we get the stronger these moments of memory become opinions.

Opinions which define to each what life means and what is to be retained as value.

With the slow slide away of yesteryear, we arrive at that moment of time when the most you have is the experience of past moments in time.

We begin to realize that the moments of speculation time have dimmed and are all but a flicker.

We now know that in older age memories and opinions constitute the most we have.

Is that so bad?

Is that not enough?

We have all those moments of past time either to keep to ourselves and reminisce or to share freely and entertain.

We can still retain to ourselves those future moments of time either to anticipate or to waste.

But the most precious moment we have is still the one right now.

The moment right now can be the opening of one's mind to a new thought or a different slant on an old one.

Or retell those old stories like old Klunkers do where they become not so old once again.

When retelling makes them young again in that past moment of time.

When old friends are present in the moment whether in fact it may not be so.

That defining moment is still the right now while we still have the right now.

It can be as effortless as noticing the glisten of frost on the morning grass or watching a sunset of changing hues.

It is as simple as realizing we are in the process of creating another day of moments of time.

The right now is the defining moment.

It is the joy of being alive and letting no one steal that joy.

It is something that is easy to talk about.

It is something that we can and should talk about even if as mundane as the weather.

The joy of living needs to exceed the pains of being alive.

The mind is still so willing even if the body, unfortunately, not so able.

We need, each in one's own way, to press the present moment into one of value.

Despite the body's frailty there has to be more than a little bit of Stephen Hawking's in each of us.

So how not to lose the joy of living?

The labored step must not be the pace we accept.

The tired mind must not set heavy on the moment.

Seek we must what Stephen has found.

Speak we must even if need be with monotone of vibrating robotics.

Now the test; now the challenge; now the quest!

It is this moment in time - the right now - that one can make another "Moment of Time" for memory sake.

What do you plan to do with your "Moment in Time" and "Those Personal Opinions"?

YOU'RE READING MINE!

TIME PASSAGES

Is it time to slow time?
Does time slip by too fast?
Time goes day by day.
Before we know it we are old.

Do we need to slow time?
Do we need to speed it up?
Truth is we can't.

A day goes with little accounting.
It goes and we let it go.
We know of yesterday.
We hope for tomorrow.
But all we have is the now of the moment.

Time is a one way slide.
No do-over.
One way and only one way.
Then for each of us all clocks stop.

Much too abruptly.
Without our consent.

No control ...no say.

Whether it be a blink or a withering away.

So what should one be doing?

Ever onward? Ever pursuing?

Race? Slow down? Enjoy?

Maybe just enough to think of it all.

Savor being here.

Fear what is to be – that infinity of time ahead.

Yet relish time's past which we know – all the happenings that came before.

The almost god-like knowing of the now and the prior.

The smugness of knowing or discovering all that was.

≈

MEDITATION

Life an anomaly or a majesty, obligated to be a self-decide.

Awareness of all extant, curiosity on the side.

How bright life's light in the crack of time; for each to become a fate divine.

Not a lord, nor a vacuum, a self-important mass of matter.

No one else can enter this body, this mind.

Careful now not self to unwind.

A dent in the warp of space, one's gravity does time hasten.

Not the before nor the after, the here and now is the prize.

Seize time by the hilt.

Lockout earth with closed eyes.

Breathe....smell...exhale.

Breathe...listen....exhale.

Think with the spirit; let now arrive.

Let contentment fill all of space.

≈

CLARION CALL

No need to be lonely when by yourself.

Illusions and delusions come to life.

Give mind to the clarion call.

Why not let the higher purpose find you.

That which we know not yet.

It surrounds this very space.

Our tiny world a mysterious place.

Set in a universe of immense extent.

Greatly exciting, more unfathomable,

beyond our reach in time and space.

We are on a path of something.

I can't imagine.

Yet thinking the purposeful glory of creation gestures from afar.

≈

EXISTENCE

Sitting silent upon an ageless stone.

Listening to the whisper of the wind.

Moving so softly past my ear.

Passing swiftly like my own existence

Telling me in passing I too will pass.

Fleeting will be my stay.

As brisk as the wind's movement sailing past.

Marking idle moments as time lost.

Gone are my footprints from Earth's eternal dust.

The wind did just erase.

Those footprints set firmly in place

Only moments before I settled here.

Why is the why of life so hard to define.
Even the path that led me here.
Those footprints nothing now but a cloud of dust.
Whirling away without a shape.

Does anything persist when peace returns?
When the winds of nature no longer stir the limbs of life.
Was there a reason?
Is there a future essence?

Go pray at the foot of the cross.
Knell before all is lost.
Only to find I know not how.
So I decided not.

≈

TIME AND FATE

We all must face the fate of time.
For each the time is short.
For some we have known, regrettably abrupt.

It matters not the years lived as the existence fulfilled.

Life is the only truth bestowed.

Not forever; none get out alive.

Only a little while here.

Like the flower to dry and float away.

Unwinding like the Grandfather clock.

Life a brief spark of light.

Bracketed by eternities of unknowing.

Billions of years now lapsed; much longer the hereafter.

Brief the mind's light between bang and black again.

Not for the before.

Not for the after.

Here and now, a lovely present and presence to have.

≈

PAUSE

Memories and knowing are here within us.

Tempered by the fear of the final dread.

Much too soon a not to be.

Life is a bit of a miracle in each of us.

So thankful and grateful to be here at all.

Not an option to look for another time or place.

Appreciate the here and now.

A sure way is to pause and savor.

Life burst alive when one is still.

Despite the pause.

Water trickles over a fall.

Leaves rustle.

Wind murmurs.

Pines whisper.

Falling stars whoosh.

≈

GONE

My thoughts so sad to hold.

Even sadder for them to be written.

Thoughts and words capture not the grief.

Each new day that early morning sun rise for me to see but not for you.

I look forward to the new day and the simple things that life brings.

The cup of coffee, the silence in the dog walk, alone in peaceful thoughts.

I skip along carried by my daily needs -the food, the air, and the clean pair of underwear.

No matter how busy I keep myself the memories find a way in.

Not an intrusion, only a reminder of someone missing.

So happy to be here; so sad not to be sharing.

I lift my head only to find I am still alone.

≈

WATCH WORDS TO AN OLD FRIEND

There comes a time when there is more to teach than there is to learn.

I'm at that time and so should you.

Do you think that you or I need to be lectured or enlightened?

Reminded of some brutish method of slaughter.

What for shock effect itself?

Man is a beast - I know that - so do you!

A lifetime of learning creates knowledge.

Knowledge leads to wisdom.

Wisdom allows good judgment.

Judgment allows one to pontificate.

There comes a time when there is more to teach then there is to learn.

≈

LIFE

On a straight stalk we bloom.

Spread our branches of thought and sight.

Lending an ear to hear whispers' from the cosmic static.

Knowing the one; understanding the zero.

Lock step with gravity on sacred dirt.

Paced by the circle of the sun.

Day to night a revolve of Earth.

Only so many ticks allotted.

So little is the area of dirt.

Not for the time before nor that hereafter.

It is the here and now that matters.

≈

SEARCH

Life is a search for the best use of the assets given at birth.
When receiving the gift of life, good fortune is not for the asking.

One's life becomes a search for the best use of the assets received.
Our role is to succeed by overcoming any deficits.

The world is a place to be investigated for what it tells us.
Start each day by making sure your head and heart are in the lead.

Everything is what it is and not some other thing.
We become today what we accomplished yesterday.

The key! Live for the moment.
Let no one steal that joy.

≈

SOLILOQUY OF ESCAPE

In one body,
Of one mind,
Short of time.

To nature,

To the stars,

To one's self be true.

≈

TURN AROUND

Turn around to face forward.

Look ahead to see where you have been.

Around again to see where you are going.

None of importance but the here and now.

Whoops no tail to grab even that has departed to another here and now.

≈

RESOLUTIONS

I am a big believer in tabula rasa, the fresh start, the virgin page.

A great way to look forward to a New Year's Day.

But I think New Year Resolutions are hocus.

We all make them.

Then break them by January 21.

Give them up.

Better luck next year.

Better to look at making life's changes on most any day.

On the day we realize a golden opportunity.

That moment of a personal epiphany.

Or that instance when doom or elation casts a thunderbolt of realization across our brow.

That is the time for maximizing MO! -MOMENTUM.

It's that small start that links things together.

Before you know it, you are roaring down life's highway with all cylinders firing.

A fresh start need not be something new.

Better to cherish that in hand, than want what is not.

Love the comfort of a broken-in shoe.

Wax the old wheels, they still don't wobble.

Dust the TV, it's not the picture, but my eyes that matter.

So what's the message?

What's my point?

Hold on to the now, that's the point!

Pull up the reins on that progressive effort to change.

Change just because things are not good enough?

What's so poor about the "now"?

What's so poor about the past?

Is what we have so poor that we should discard as trash?

Should those we know and love be forgotten and not thought of?

Should old times past and lessons learn to be ignored?

We should retain and conserve old times and old friends.

We should toast them now and always.

We should keep them close and not liberate them into the trash bins of change.

What can be more pleasant than our family and friends?

Let me be on the list of old acquaintances you should never forget.

≈

AGED

AN OLD MAN'S LAMENT 44
ODE TO THE OLD 45
GRIEVING THE LOSS OF DREAMS 47
EVER IN BETWEEN 51
DECLINING YEARS 52
TODAY 54
DAY DREAMING GONE 56
MEMORIES 59
NIGHT MOOD 60
STRUCTURED SLEEP 61
ALZHEIMER'S 62
DEPARTURE 64
AS TIME GETS NEAR 67
USE-BY-DATE 69
BACKING UP 70
OLD AGE 71
SPICE 71
SIGNS 72
SELF ABUSE 72
WHAT OLD BRINGS TO THE TABLE 73
HUMOR 74
LITTLE DOUBT 74

≈

AGED

Age is life's inescapable measurement.

Young age has a component of immortality.

Middle age vigorously grasping all opportunities.

Old age thankfulness and wisdom.

Regrettably, we pay little attention to age until we are aged.

It becomes time for true appreciation and to establish reality.

Frailty finally recognized; the meaning of finite brackets consciousness.

How each of us handles life becomes to each his own.

So be it.

Don Erdek

AN OLD MAN'S LAMENT

I waddle when I walk.
No sprint of step.
No fleet of foot.
I waddle when I walk.

I mumble when I talk.
No yarn to spin.
No gift of gab.
I mumble when I talk.

I squint when I look.
No gleam of eye.
No clarity of vision.
I squint when I look.

I "what" when I listen.
No words are heard.
No repeats loud enough.
I "what" when I listen.

I think I know when I think.
No thoughts come quickly.

No actions follow thought.
I think I know when I think.

I waddle when I walk.
I mumble when I talk.
I squint when I look.
I "what" when I listen.
I think I know when I think.
I wonder just how much further I can sink.

≈

ODE TO THE OLD

I am an old man.
A very old man.
I am old enough to call myself old.

I know I look old.
I know I walk old.
I know my body is thoroughly worn out.
My face sag tells it all.

I have been around for a long time.
Actually I like that.

I know right from wrong.
I know good from evil.
It comes with living long.

I know things.
I know things the young do not know.
I hope they will someday learn the things I know.

I know sincerity.
I know relevance.
I am confident in what I know.

I have no axe to grind.
My axe is fine honed by the emery of experience.
Gleaned by years of looking and listening and learning.
It's called knowledge.

So what is it that I know?
I know I am every person who is old.
I know we don't count any more.
I know our knowledge is considered old.
I may like to talk, but so much more I want to be heard.

I have no powers or gift of gab for crowd adulation.

I am the grandfathers and grandmothers of America.

We are the ones that still so cherish our life.

Our life of hard work and solid morals.

You see, our life also started with hope and change.

So little resemblance to that of today.

Bent on trashing so much of what we created.

We know that are lives were relevant and progressive.

Standard of living bears witness to that.

We did the best we could.

Improve on the best; let go of the rest.

≈

GRIEVING THE LOSS OF DREAMS

Blessed enough to grow old.

Aged years carry losses.

Lost loved ones, pets, jobs, relationships and a good bit of health.

Greatest and simplest of them all, the loss of who we once were.

Back in youth there were no wrinkles.

None except the laugh lines from a beaming smile.

Girls with their spontaneous youthful giggle.

The female body in full bloom, all by itself.

The guys dreaming of sliding into home plate.

Hitting a home run.

Catching a pass on a dead run.

The jump shot ---all net.

Climbing to the top of a tree.

More friends than ever again.

Sharing the learning curve with other fresh faces.

Having happy dreams, youthful and original.

But here we are today.

No longer able to leap tall buildings.

Even a set of stairs is a push.

Thinning of hair puts more meat on our head.

We now have an affinity and sympathy for the color gray.

And if not the graying of hair it is the loss there of.

What bothers us most are the things we once could do but no longer can.

As the years pass the toll mounts.

Those losses of dreams make us sad.

The vitality of youth is now long gone.

The loss of looks and the weight gain.

The loss of muscle tone and the walk that is now a shuffle.

The eyesight and loss of hearing.

The memory lapses and the "just can't remember".

It's the knowing of what once was a could, has now become a can't.

It's the knowing that we never can again.

It makes us sad ...it shouldn't...but it does.

Getting old is not an option; it's not a choice.

It sure as hell or heaven beats the alternate.

It's good to be here stumble walking, mumble talking, squinty seeing and hardly hearing.

So now we find ourselves happy with another day.

Hoping to see another Christmas, another New Year.

Painfully enduring rap and hip-hop.

So what to do when dreams no longer are true?

Complain not about getting old.

We still can be pleased with what we once did and once could do.

For we are so much wiser and secure with who we now are.

We are strong of thought and firm of conviction.

Gained in patience but no longer feel a need to be pleasantly understanding.

Yes, we lost a lot, but gained so much more.

The gain of so many life experiences is rewarding if we but accept them as such.

Every day should bring them back to the mind's eye and enjoy those times again.

It is an easy fix to remake bad memories into a lesson learned.

The richness of maturity is the accumulation of memories.

What is needed is to package them differently.

The difference being the contrast between youth and maturity.

Back in our youth we were so tender and fresh.

We should find it easy to remember those many innocent faces.

Back then when most all were awkward and shy.

Release some of your staunchly held independence and be a bit more dependent.

Really, it's not that bad and not that hard to do.

No telling what mischief and secrets can still be found in an aging body and mind.

So much to cherish in each new rise of the morning sun.

Ah hell!, we all wish we could be eighteen again.

EVER IN BETWEEN

I never dreamed I'd live to see the ancient age of 83.
When action at its best is a shaky hand, a staggered step;
Regretful of the chances not taken.
So many ambitions left vacant.

It's depressing to know I'm old.
Despite visionary starts, actions fell short.
Some jubilant years of health and wealth.
Now dashed in aged twilight.

How did I get here so fast?
Where did the years go?
My youth slipped silently away, middle years zipped by.
It was the constant now that ever forced to intervene.

Much too often in a slump.
Some not easily shaken off.
Trying to believe self is still a part of human's team.
Wondering how many more days to play a genuine part.

You and I are forever in between.
Each day another uncertain dream.

A past behind, a look ahead.

Via default, today will find its own solitary way.

Advise self not to dream.

Try instead to rely on inner strength.

Do not dwell on one poor thing, or hope for a doubtful other.

Steel the mind, adapt to willowing time.

What then the current concern.

Is it how or if we will be missed?

Terrible thought! Stay in the present; regain control.

Command something larger of the frail body.

We are not forever young. Ever somewhere in between.

≈

DECLINING YEARS

No ties, nothing serious.

No lifetime commitments

Lifetime is all but run.

Only today, this hour, the right now to be won.

Ask not for long term commitment.
Long term is not in the offer.
Look not for oaths, pledges,
or promises of love everlasting.
Be satisfied with giggles and laughs for however long they last.

Knowing not what comes next.
Unsure the meaning of duration.
Only the now to sport.
Unknowing when life may short circuit or abort.

So find joy in the life.
The living in the moment.
Find reason to laugh,
Tickle a fancy.
Find a feather tickle another.

Listen for music.
The music to dance.
Dance with the declining years.
What better than friendship and giving fun one last chance

≈

Don Erdek

TODAY

Sadness that thoughts no longer resonate with the many others.

Critical of the forced direction taken into dependency.

Disappointed in judgments made that deeply affect a good life.

Worried about moral issues that trivialize goodness.

Much that just not right, and in fact down-right wrong.

Or as with most issues, lacking a search for truth.

Political correctness that prevails and distorts any choice of wisdom.

Is this aged me, just too old and of little use.

Yet I know so much.

Have seen so much.

Lived long.

Very long.

When does living very long become too long?

I have developed common sense to the level of un-commonality.

I've made enough mistakes to clearly know what is not right at a glance.

Years of travel has cured me of certain vanities.

So much to be said of the wisdom of age.

Yet being ignored is often a glaring and pointed reminder.

So disappointing to be considered too old to be listened to.

So powerless for opinions to gain traction.

So unable to transfer knowledge gained and wisdom garnered to the youth who lack the same.

I guess I need to find new challenges.

Find goals that match my passions.

Things that make me feel good about myself

TV, E-Mails and Facebook ain't gonna do it.

I want to be challenged.

There had come that time for a change; but that was a while ago.

Whether necessary or not, some things need come to pass.

Age was a factor; Economics begged consideration.

Health was pushing the reality button.

Change and less independence became a transition into a slow ease back.

Much less of future time for the outdoors

The indoors an ambiance required to master.

All became a series of decisions taking a long time to develop hopefully.

Worse of it all there is no new stuff.

The self has so little to contribute.

To lose one's sense of worth is bitter.

I no longer conquer new challenges.

I don't relish the fact that I don't have to work anymore.

I miss doing something meaningful.

Sooner, not later, I'm going to need more.

≈

DAY DREAMING GONE

Maybe it's a good time to dream.

No! Old people don't dream any more.

They reminisce.

When did that happen?

When did that become necessary?

When did daydreams become reminiscing?

It didn't happen overnight.

It didn't happen just yesterday.

It happened without a sign.

Daydreaming just melted away.

Youthful daydreaming was a free flight of the mind.

When one tells oneself I'm gonna ease back and dream a while.

Just a few moments for mental wandering.

For what ends?

None really, just something to defy planning.

Most happen serendipitously.

Just something not to do.

Daydreaming unleashes the brain for a random walk away from anything real.

It is something that requires no movement of the limbs.

Akin to a neon balloon floating up, up, and away into the waiting sky.

Summertime always the ideal season for a fresh grass flop.

Looking skyward at slow moving clouds with no tick or tock of time.

But OH! How it has changed with time.

Or might it be but an aging mind that has left fifty or sixty years slide by.

Daydreams seem to have faded from the mind.

Replaced by a different mind wandering ...One of reminiscing.

The reality of the past now replaces the wishful thinking that once whisked through our youthful mind's sweet wanderings.

Now when idle moments arise, we remember old friends, old faces, old places and days gone by.

Friends and foes become subjects of fleeting fantasy in the mind's eye.

The remembrances are now partly true, part embellished, but mostly contrived.

Daydreams once were like the free air of the future with so much room and time for breathing.

Reminiscing and reverie are now like a Bourbon on ice with the richness of the past to savor.

In daydreams there was only that free spirit of happiness.

With remembrance there comes sorrow.

Remembrance too often becomes sadness of lost family.

Those thoughts cause gloom to descend and smiles to depart.

We remember opportunities missed, crosses that we bore, errant words to those close.

AH! More regrets then hopes.

All too many poor performances.

Too many wishes unfulfilled.

Too many want to do over.

Not enough reality of what's done is done.

We remember too many awful truths about ourselves.

There are no do over.

We can, at times, be harder on ourselves than any other.

MEMORIES

We worry about time.

When young we had a future.

Now being old it is the past that captures our idle moments.

When young, time is not important, the future is far away.

With age, the pendulum swing draws attention, gravity holds sway.

Death's figure shortens future's path; dark shadows shade the way.

And yet, who should regret all the memories.

Must savor the richness of a life long-lived.

Having done so much and lived so long, it is hard to remember it all.

So do we focus on only a few?

Even the highs and lows of the past are too many.

Not time enough given to relive our memories.

They possess a richness like no other; having taken a lifetime to accumulate.

Must certainly remember, all those memories belong to me.

It is a possession like no other.

Refreshing to know that every other has their own.

Don Erdek

NIGHT MOOD

Here in stoic silence, sleep not found.

Lingering in a pensive, repentant, purgatorial mood.

Still so early in the AM.

Dark outside.

Not a star to be seen...there must be a cloud shroud to hide them all.

Not a thing moving, almost scary.

Not a sound to be heard, almost eerie.

Not a soul around.

Even the wind is silent, no need to move.

Only me and my reverie.

The night is the hardest time to be alive and 4AM knows all my secrets.

A time for inner gloom and outer reflection.

Reflecting upon past deeds and future needs.

Those deeds done well and those poorly performed.

The pressure of age bearing down on a body whose youthful tone left so long ago.

The desire to have it back; knowing that can never be.

Accepting the body's aging loss.

Replacing the loss with a gratitude for the days past and for each new one to be given.

≈

STRUCTURED SLEEP

Structured sleep should no longer be important to the retired.

Sleep a waste of time.

At least a waste of time left.

Believe it or not we should regard sleep as a squandering of the finite time available.

We should no longer be bound by schedules or the ding-ding of a clock or an alarm.

No longer by daylight or darkness.

We should command time and not let it happen the other way around.

No work schedules.

No tossing and turning only because it is dark outside.

No lying awake.

We should sleep only when we want to and not be bracketed by daylight.

Isn't it great not to be limited by time to do or not to do as we wish?

Retirement relieves the confines of time - schedule are fluid.

Time to do things become, "only when I want to".

What's strange or maybe not so strange is when I'm home in my own space I indeed can control time.

When I go out into the world time is controlled, re: opening and closing times, business hours of Post Office, restaurants, etc.

So sleep should only be if we want to or the body or the mind tells to do.

Naps are the greatest institution for the retired.

A nap should be renamed as a map - Meditation and Planning.

This works really well, because we can.

≈

ALZHEIMER'S

The dawn fades as life's sunset appears.

No flags, no signs, no thresholds to guide.

With stealth, with age, with a shadowy cloak the dotage darkens.

Alzheimer's invades without a sound.

So quiet it steals the memory.

I don't remember that event.

I can't recall that predicament.

The senses dull in non-response.

The passion now lost; no longer to find.

Emotions slack and slaked by time.

Why remember if there is no need.
Why retain an experience, a happening, a thought, if it is of no use.
Old memories like old clothes simply don't fit.

Alzheimer's a loss of memory or a loss of a need to remember.
For you see it is more than a closet of old clothes that don't fit.
It is the "it" in the "fit" that fits no more.
That move to self-darkness of not knowing me.

It is the "it" that sees not the aging me.
The "it" senses not the onset of senility.
The "it" accepts this siege without a whimper, without a fight.

"It" knows of staggering steps, the loss of sight.
"It" senses the quaking hand, the strain to hear.
But the "it" shies away from the worst to fear - the loss of who I am.

Anxiety may precede the loss of knowing.
Horror of not knowing when the who I am no longer knows.
A burden to not know who I am but more so for them that know.
A tragedy for family.
A pity to friends.

A total unawareness most likely for me.

Dread and sorrow, a failure to cope, ensnares those others.

The me to be oblivious of the darkness descending on me.

My heart, my breath will strain for survival.

My departing mind gives not a clue that the body no longer has a thoughtful thing to do.

≈

DEPARTURE

So rich with awareness is life today.

Hard to grasp this entity will decay.

Is a coup de grace set for the Elysian Field or a debarking on Stygian shore?

There is no reason that I be spared.

No amount of sorrow to create a return.

A return to what? When more time is never enough.

death's winged chariot draws near.

Each aging year multiplies the fear.

The bomb of death it carries.

A missile so lethal as to reduce self to dust in its wake.

There is no announcement on its timing.

No notice of departure when it arrives. It spreads its cold terror even as life is lived.

We are born and become aware of a lineage before to create the me.

They, whoever they may be, started back a long time ago.

Not as old as Earth but in time and on its surface united.

There was an immensity of time before without the me.

A lineage of others who persisted in creation.

A great and wonderful line of humanity specific to me.

As well as another line for you.

And who knows how far back it was the same two.

Way, way back in time, absolute and for sure, two mature individuals did copulate.

Then again and again, and again, two others.

Always and for sure one male and one female did procreate.

Each mature; each fertile.

Every generation, willing or not.

Every ancestor beyond the biology of childhood.

No generation ever skipped; no immaculate conceptions.

So it is I am here and so are you.

The absence of you and me in years before tilts the mind to where was self?

How can that be if now we breathe?

Where were we, was it somewhere in space or a yet to matter.

Matter can neither be created nor destroyed, so the scientists say.

Perish the thought of where our matter will be later.

Or doesn't it really matter.

Truly if it doesn't matter, why don't I want my matter to depart.

I know not one thing of finite years before I was here.

Where was I? Was it in those who once were here?

Was I somewhere in an empty space or there in pieces of some far flung matter.

During the Ice Age, did two survive.

In Caesar's time what was my place and who were those two?

The plague was not theirs nor my extermination.

And their thoughts are they now my thoughts.

Where now is the matter of those who once were here?

I must bear witness and do them honor.

Respect and show true gratitude.

Yet I have no remembrance of the time before, nor the life they lived.

I see them not, so will the future also not see me.

Are we to be no more than a tombstone dash between birth and requiem?

In Elysian Field to lie in an abode of the blessed after death.

Showing the full of life we lived as but a dash.

A dash to sum it all can never prove meaningful or do justice to one's existence.

The dark woods of death will snare us all.

Sooner or later.

What about the later.

Will it be a peaceful last sleep?

Or perhaps a greater than life adventure.

≈

AS TIME GETS NEAR

As time gets near, is there a time to say goodbye?

Everyone has a hard time trying to say it.

Others don't want to hear it.

So it seems it is something not likely to be said

No words are sounded; no words wanting to be heard.

There must be a way to avoid the morose.

There must be a way for one not to cause others to weep.

How to leave and relay that life was good.

We all know life is never forever.

How to grasp before-hand that event when self and others avoid and shun its reality.

Why do we not want to discuss that the life lived, was lived well.

How do we discuss a topic which cannot be discussed after the fact?

To be born is to face the end.

Is there a message that one can derive from Nobel?

An obituary written prematurely moved him to create a legacy of enduring value.

Is it possible to let others know how pleased one is to have lived.

One that can be said with truth and sincerity by communicating "Please don't weep for me"

There must be a way to say "No matter how much I'd like to stay ...I can't".

You have no way to change that fact.

No matter how you wish to, the trip is only for me to take.

There is no law of nature that allows for mortality.

Everyone wants to go to heaven; but no one wants to go today.

Yet like Nobel we could take the time to make things right.

In fact tackling one's own obituary might lead to improvement.

No telling what we may choose to do in the last decade or two.

I wonder why we don't treat demise with some form of magnanimity.

If life was a good one who better to honor the life lived but the one who lived it.

That one who knows it all with all the intimate details, passions, virtues and wrongs as well as loves.

Now making believe that demise is far off and not of concern is one way to go.

I'm not preoccupied with this subject but as you can tell I use the word "demise" and not the other "D" word.

So it seems I am at a point of massive confusion and find this subject most peculiar.

But let's get real and personal.

I want smiles on the faces of my kids.

I want them to know their dad.

They don't have to think like me or even agree with me.

I gave them as much as I could.

I want I like you "Pop-Pop" on the lips of my Grandkids.

I want them to know who I was and what I did.

To Brothers and Friends, and any that care "The road we shared was more than enough."

≈

USE-BY-DATE

Now is my time to worry.

My better years are behind.

Old age has taken its toll on my body.

Liberalism and progressive idealism has taken its toll on my mind.

Cost of living has taken a toll on my self-respect to provide for myself.

Today I can earn no more; yet expected to pay more for health and all of life's essentials.

My mind has omits and blanks of unusable thought pockets.

Hope is hard to find and improvement elusive.

Forward a myth when the pole star of prosperity is lost in political correctness and sense of entitlement.

But what do I know.

I'm already several years past my "Use-by-date".

≈

BACKING UP

Lazy body, lazy mind.

Many older adults are unmotivated.

They make time for television, video games and social media.

Most sit a lot and do minimum to get by.

There is little potential.

No desire to light the fire of motivation.

Doing nothing is the best thing to do.

Get out of reverse.

Gas up and drive.

≈

OLD AGE

Old age has its ups and downs.

Once it was a body committed only to the way up.

Now mostly the way down sifting through life's scrapes.

Patching the body with the duct tape of medication.

Each day, a day of sameness.

The evening ends too soon with a weariness of frame.

Even though little was done of that which can tire.

≈

SPICE

What was stable is now a shaky.

What was bustle is now lethargy.

What was chaos is now inactivity.

It is when life reaches the point of no longer giving.

The start of take away.

The possible begins to curve to the improbable.

When the future is today and today needs spice.
Expecting providence to rush in.
Hoping intelligence will not be denied.

Moments when it feels like joy is no longer to be.
And then something changes.
And it happens.

≈

SIGNS

I wonder is it another sign of old age or is it a sign of the times.
Those decisions to make do rather than buy new.

≈

SELF ABUSE

As I grow older I become less active.
My body is weak and worn from long use.
I rely on what I learned to see me through the rest of the journey.
Often I feel life has been drained of color, interest and pleasure.
My mind has atrophied as well.
Not from overuse but from disregard.

Youthful curiosity has succumbed to thoughtless neglect.

Barely noticing I have become a little duller - a bit dimmer.

≈

WHAT OLD BRINGS TO THE TABLE

This might now be the time to think.

To reminisce, to be painfully honest.

The time to tap the wealth of your intelligence.

For conscience to tease forth eternal truths.

Study your inner sanctum; it's the treasure chest of one's life.

A wealth made for you by you.

There is within cached accounts to refine.

Hidden but saved for value you saw in life gone by.

Uncover, retrieve those gems of worth laid carefully aside.

You know today all you have done and not taken time enough to survey.

Lay them bare upon mind's table.

Access, assess and uncloak the answers to the wonder of all creation - yourself.

HUMOR

Old age is a fine time for humor.

A time when humor is harder to find.

Yet the time when it is needed the most.

A time when all you've ever done - the right, the wrong - is here.

It is also the time when all you hoped to do but didn't do is not here.

≈

LITTLE DOUBT

Let us have little doubt.

That you have a rendezvous with destiny.

Till then you have the ability and the agility.

To challenge time.

You have that at your disposal.

Until the dash is chiseled into a tombstone.

Until debarking on the shore of River Styx.

There resides a fight to live.

Below the basal carpe diem.

Above the zone of quantum foam.

Resides a will set free with umbilical snip.

A release to elegance.

Immortality is not a given.

Nor is eternal youth.

Everyday life is too precious for casual regard.

Joy to live is self-create.

≈

LIGHT

UNINSPIRED FLING 79
DAYDREAMING 80
WHERE DO DAY DREAMS GO? 82
JOYLESS HURT 84
FEEL FREE TO FLEE 86
CLAIM 87
GENOME 88
THE MOTHER SCAR 90
FREE WILL 93
APOLOGY 94
THE EDGE 95
FINDING HONESTY ON SQUARE POND 96
SQUINT 97
LOVE 98
SWEET NOVEMBER 98
AFTER GLOW 100
TWO GLASSES OF WINE 101
ESCAPE 102
SOLO 105
JESTER 106
BONES 109
BLUNDER 109
CHANGE 110
"I" 110

ROAD SAGE 110
AVERAGE 111
TEMPERAMENT 111
COMMODE 111
MUSINGS 112

≈

LIGHT

Life is like a neon balloon.

Hold firmly the string lest it escapes.

Cherish its lightness, the buoyancy it possesses.

The colorfulness added each day.

The flexibility of its skin reacting to the vagrancies of space.

With the smoothness of transition, it floats within the dimension of time and space.

Its lightness and brightness qualifying a well-lived life.

UNINSPIRED FLING

Damn this life.

Damn its empty existence.

I once was young, you know.

What was the purpose, the destiny...it seems to have passed me by.

These waters I see before me I don't understand, I'm sure they in turn care not for me.

So let this solitary bay deal with this shabby hat that I cast away in distress.

I have become a sea apart from human understanding and a universe of separation from the answer to why.

I seek not reciprocity, agreement or amnesty.

My body sags limp inside baggy pants, my mind downcast,
I'm saddened by a departure of faith.

Alone in mind, frozen in snapshot time.

The now of soft water is lapping at my feet, inexplicably soothing my uninspired woes.

It's not my age that hampers nor the white of hair.

It is the unknowing of my genesis in a universe guided by entropy that speeds evermore rapidly to empty.

What is my destiny? Do I ever get to know?

So alone I remain frozen in photographic poise, eyes and head downcast in despair.

Yet in defiance the might of my right arm rebels and flings my hat.

Could it be my reverie searching for some time before or possibly a better heavenly after?

I'll wait a moment before I look up to see if that hat will float away or chance a route of return.

Life is but happenstance with a probability ring.

So will my mindless hat, by gentle wave-assist, return to me or slowly drift away without a solitary care?

Returning a sign to hope and pray; drifting away a sign to remain apart in an uninspired way.

≈

DAYDREAMING

Far, far, away, how our minds do stray.

Leaving reality away from the now.

Across time and space our thoughts skip away.

Daydreaming unleashes the mind.

A random walk from anything real.

No movement of the limbs required.

No limit to what we ponder.

No perimeter on the subject.

It's a pause for nothing but eye's-wide-open dreaming.

Like a neon balloon floating up, up, up and away, into a waiting sky.

As free as air between here and the horizon.

Freedom for an idle mind to chase a wandering muse.

Daydreams are idle thoughts and bits of curiosity.

Imagination unleashed instantaneously to run wild.

Or in the next instance bundled into ingenuity with a search for genesis.

Nary a thought held long enough to settle.

The mind equally open for valued thoughts or useless nonsense.

As featureless as a smooth ocean or as choppy as wind tossed waves.

Summertime the ideal season for a fresh grass flop.

Looking skyward at slow moving swells of clouds.

Leaving the body in limbo.

Free flight of the mind so special in youthful years.

When one's virgin self tells the inner being to ease.

Releasing the mind to nature's breeze.

Daydreaming about something you would like to have, but never might.

A prince charming, a companion with class, winning the lottery.

A carefree wonderful life, lots of happiness but little strife.

A fantasy world where sense and perfection do not prevail.

Maybe to look for that grand plan, a destiny, or pursue the big picture.

Then again nothing at all, but this wonderful, wandering pipe dream.

≈

WHERE DO DAYDREAMS GO?

Where do daydreams go?

Often back to a happier time; but sometimes on to the future and an expectation.

To an existence without stress, leaving responsibility behind.

As life slides by, there arises more vividness within those day dreams.

The "me" is always the main actor of importance... the star...the Walter Mitty!

Filled with glory and fame.

Giddiness and happiness seep on in.

Embarrassment and pleasure come in waves.

Those daydreams become a place where the body need not go.

Where only thought need exist.

And all thoughts going with the flow; going where the lonely go.

A pause in life and a departure to mind's space.

Unzipping the cosmos, eclipsing time...going where no one else can know.

Not the age or aged body daunts the transit.

On to discover the mystery of indigo.

Day breaks...night falls.

Our perceptions of the world emerge.

Our passions and desires manifold.

Our triumphs and defeats become repeats.

Sweetness overcomes any bitterness of the whole human experience.

Nothing like a somnambulistic moment.

So kick back on a bench or sprawl in the grass it's what in essence means to be free.

≈

Don Erdek

JOYLESS HURT

Don't let anyone steal your joy.
Finding joy comes not easy.
Requires courage and fortitude and self-reliance.

Courage to search for truth.
Fortitude to believe in yourself.
Self-reliance to carry it out.

Ironic is it not!
The person you most adore,
the thing you most enjoy,
they can be the most woe-some.

The one closest,
the thing most loved,
that one adored,
to these your joy exposed.
Most apt to steal your joy.

The fault is trusting.
The vulnerability is self-exposure.

Trust not.

Protection required.

How and who might pierce the unguarded veil?

That satin wrap around your soul called love.

A shroud not of armor but amour.

Might not appreciation of exposure be in order.

A trusting soul so weak as not expecting harm.

A naïve desire to be desired.

That search for understanding and affection so open to sincere or possible insincere affection.

The higher the lift; the harder the fall.

That which comes last endures longer, digs deeper, hurts harsher.

The deeper the love; the lonelier the abyss.

Misery that brings one to the knees.

The solace offered.

Better to have loved than never loved at all.

Bleeding heart platitudes do little to placate.

Happy faces and Emojis placate not.

Putting a happy face on sorrow is like ice cream on a ghost pepper.

Blame not others.

The fault lies within.

It is I who glorified the life lived while ignoring any sorrow which might follow.

Might the culprit be self.

Might it be that no one steals our joy.

We leave it exposed to be taken for granted.

≈

FEEL FREE TO FLEE

In this life I've learned a lot about human nature.

People most everywhere are kind, generous and good.

Regardless of where I lived there have been similar likes, dislikes and desires.

The best things happen without planning.

Life is like a long highway.

Each of us thumbing a ride to open adventure.

You just have to go with it.

Wherever it takes you.

There is an adventure down any road taken.

A mystery with each person encountered.

Around the next bend is innocent discovery.

Random events at most every speed.

At the next stop, life changing meetings.

Your boulevard maybe tree lined or rocky.

Chance upon a unexpected scene.

Meet someone to share a dream.

The key no planning required.

Twist not nor censor any episode.

Go with the flow, shoot any bump.

Stop only to slake a thirst.

Pause only to charge the internal battery.

It's your life it's uppa to you to live it.

CLAIM

On a globe of dirt there resides a race.

Their only place in all of space.

They lay claim to the heavens.

That be but ego speak.

The vastness they are aware.

In haughtiness laying claim as theirs to share.

This race has a soul or so it thinks.

Civilization and the endeavor to persevere their road to fame.

But wars and killing belies the claim.

How self-serving.

How egotistical.

How self-centered.

All cloaked in self-importance and impiety.

≈

GENOME

Genome is given at birth.

From Father and Mother endowed.

There upon inoculated with the elixir of life.

Set free to seek a singular path.

Genome tells not the heart to beat.

What to hear, nor that to listen to.

The eyes to blink, nor the image to capture.

The mind to think, nor belief to hold on to.

Chromosomes and genes delegate, albeit choose not to mandate.

Personality, intelligence, looks and nature set with flexible precision.

Free will unleashed by the umbilical snip.

Learning and memory an individual effort to attain.

Choose wisely; push the boundary.

Do more than merely exist.

One must adapt, change, respond.

The pattern is set; the color, the flavor is not.

A nature to nurture ever the conflict.

One must adapt, change, respond.

Emotions not so plain,

as amino acids aside a helical sugar phosphate chain.

To a surprising extent the genome determines.

To a greater degree it is what we learn.

The genes provide the tools.

The skill to use is self-taught

≈

Don Erdek

THE MOTHER SCAR

The one and only connect - the Mother Scar.
A tattoo from past existence.
The seal and sealing of individuality.

Remains of a temporal connect.
A lifeline severed at partition.
Each cast to individual self.

Naked into an oxygen sea.
Never ever to again be totally connected.
On one's own but not alone.

Initiated by father.
A tube latch to mother.
Linked to ancestors.

To all those earlier.
Those that survived the perils before.
Never an abort the making of unique you.

The DNA die was set by intercourse injection.
Genes were cast.

Formation the final test.

Mother's belly a cozy nest.

Nature sets the human term limit at thirty-five.

Time enough to feed and grow.

By oneself with mother's help

Failure is natures natural abort.

Father the seed to sprout the egg.

Genes to provide a pattern.

Mother the genesis, a womb to grow.

Placenta a paternal fence to protect.

Heart to beat.

Parts to grow.

Brain first then all the rest.

Genetic character imbued upon liquid fuel ignition. Like a living missile, burning until partition.

Natal fire bloom with development.

Separation called for by completion.

Into the air-surround world with nothing on.

The body formed, the brain nothing in.

On one's own the strive to live.

A breath taken.

The taste for existence.

Is solo to feel.
Together with those you hear.

Where I came from, not a clue.

Life a mystery.

The Mother Scar a cluster bump.

The belly button, a sign of when I came to be.

The mark to start my strive.

The will to stay alive.

Sutured sign shows true partition.

Showing begot from another.

The mark of start of solo strive.

The wonderful will to stay alive.

An anti-entropic; non-chaotic force.

A path to destiny and perfection.

Reclaiming destiny's intention.

Reversing a Big Bang point of destruction.

Be not flippant when contemplating your naval.

Allow more than idle thinking.

Think not waste of time.

Penetrate to deepest reflection of self in space and time.

That connection, once direct.

The naval, a physical sign.

DNA, the pattern from before.

The mental, the senses, the will to survive.

Seek answers to mighty self-questions.

What is life?

Why was I born?

Was it magic or Vegas odds - the sperm select?

How do I honor the gift begot?

≈

FREE WILL

Free will is the freedom to think or not.

To stand on one's own two feet or not.

To be confident in oneself or not.

To live life to its fullest or not.

To work or not.

To be of value or not.

To succeed or not.

To love or not.

To love oneself or not.

To be virtuous or not.

To blame others or not.

To do nothing or not.

Let no one steal your free will.

Let no one steal your joy.

APOLOGY

To be human is to err.
The good sometimes sin.
The bad often sin.
The evil want to sin.

What may be a proper correction for a wrongdoing?
An apology is the accepted route.
What then is a proper apology?

"I'm sorry" doesn't get it.
A true and meaningful apology requires four steps for acceptance.
Step one is a true recognition within one's self that a wrong has been committed.
Step two is indeed to apologize with words or actions that are

sincere; "I'm sorry" is more often not enough.

Step three is to provide restitution to satisfy the wrong as fully and humanly as possible.

Step four. Never ever repeat the sin... which by default constitutes an apology negation.

≈

THE EDGE

God was responsible for getting things up and running.

But after that not so much.

So hard to appreciate the creation of a cosmic horizon.

The start and end of it all.

The far, far out edge of an observable universe.

Creation's beginning and nothingness final frontier.

An edge where we may never know what lies beyond.

The rush away of matter.

The limit of light to record the recede.

Human frailty or God's intent to deceive.

Did he create us with a limitation not to know it all.

≈

Don Erdek

FINDING HONESTY ON SQUARE POND

Truth is in the whisper of the wind,
The waves upon a sandy shore,
The haunting cry of a distant loon,
The soft patter of leaves falling at night upon the roof.

It is the feel of sand beneath the feet,
The warmth of the rising sun,
The stars of an ebony night,
The flicker of the flame at a companionless campfire.

Truth is the surest help in a time of need.
It is as awesome as the setting sun.
As green as the distant trees across Square Pond.
As simple as a baby's smile when wet water touches its skin.

It is as explosive as a pounding heart,
As quiet as a breath in restful sleep,
As seeking as a soul longing for appreciation,
As truthful as God exists in unity with all creation...
not separate from it.

≈

SQUINT

I remember when first we met.

In Saudi Arabia some two score and six.

Your smile captured me.

It portrayed a awesome warmth with eyes that squint.

That squint is no longer distant.

I see it now close and often.

Close enough to share wonderful memories.

Some lost long ago; others stowed away waiting for today.

Together we joy in the unwrapping.

Those memories of bygone times, foreign places and long ago friends.

We unwind those ribbons that bind.

Ribbons of love and happiness.

Might this be a meant to be?

Or was memory of a squinting eye that set it free.

LOVE

Love is like a wave upon the ocean.

Ever gentle.

Slow in undulation.

Rising and falling to feelings.

Stirred by carnal currents.

Crashing in extremum upon a shoal of acceptance.

≈

SWEET NOVEMBER

An old friend.

A special friend.

When time and circumstance intersect.

Fate finds passage to fill with affection.

November, the edge of a year.

Aged, the twilight of sensuality.

The wrinkles of time challenge libido.

Passion like smoke through a keyhole finds essence in space.

Sweet November, a month for making a meant to be into reality.

Pondering origins, pursuing destiny.

Knowing what is not meant to continue won't.

Behaving well, seldom makes for joy.

Like drab autumn leaves, the brilliance all but expired.

The bud, the bloom, the sweet perfume, not meant to last a lifetime.

The sag of body, the bent of frame, fools not the eye of beauty.

The now of sweet November striped and hooked like a candy cane.

The pause in time, a Luray of caves, a traffic jam, beloved old Savannah.

Music, laughter, a physical presence, candy to sweeten November urge.

White sweet soft snow plows the drive around a treasured lake.

Creating memory footprints like endearing nights aloft to remember.

A steady beat of heart intervenes and aspires.

Honey kisses a mead to purr and coo or monkey hugs, fingers meant to woo.

November, thirty days of pleasure and gratification.

Joys, excitement, like beads of pearls strung with sincere affection.

A jujube of pure delight.

Months or years, a finite number of days.

Sweetness, not the sole property of November.

True love to be captured in many ways.

≈

AFTER GLOW

Lying in sweet surrender.

Not yet yielding to slumber.

Not here, not there.

Somewhere floating down.

After the climax of sexual pleasure.

Following the burst of primordial exuberance.

The release return of sheer delight.

Lust and love no need to parse.

Rushing to climax with directions from above.

A climb to ecstasy.

All movement and positioning.

The delirium of the moment driven by love's passion.

A brain zone of primitive desire.

The zest for life to recreate.

More likely sheer delight.
Beyond rational and reason.
Thirst for immortality the hidden drive.

Being spurned on to culminate.
No thought, no decision.
Transcending extinction by the joy of nirvana.
Bursting beyond the heat of passion.
Attaining saturated satisfaction.

Somewhere floating down in final beatitude.
Oblivious to pain, care or reality.
A goal hoped for and attained.
After glow.

≈

TWO GLASSES OF WINE

One C K Mondavi; the other White Zin.
Not Love Birds; two distinct individuals.
Finding joy roosting on a bar stool.

A companionship of mutual respect for living in the moment.
Pleasure in small talk, often broken by giggles and laughs.
Some time for the serious and mundane.

More than a bit for nonsense.

Holding hands a sign of ease.

To others outward affection; to them a personal connection.

More than a handshake or a peck on the cheek.

An appreciation of dearly sought closeness.

Enjoying renewed vitality beyond the wine.

Sub-rosa the massaging fingers create thrills of delight.

Naked fingers express a secret reality.

White and pink the glasses clink.

The lips of the two often meet.

The edge of the glass or each other.

≈

ESCAPE

How intricate the spider weaves it's web.

How complex the design.

How stealth the snare.

A betrothal scheme, a connived carnal carousel.

A sensual love net lustfully spun with feminine charm.

Meant to entangle and strangle for creation sake.

The spider, a beauty, an hourglass of enchanting delight.

Possessing all the hex and jinx an enchantress aspires to possess.

Bewitch the lure; the web the hook.

The spider waits...Its plans made...It's design fashioned.

Unable to help herself, unable to slake matriarchal demands.

Unable, incapable, unwilling to judge life's value to that of the seed even when seed has proved to be lacking.

The web is her weave woven of silken lustful thread spun from that same womb of conception.

The spider waits...silently yet hidden ready to pounce.

Sinister gusts of evil pass through; they neither shake nor stir.

Her plots and plans are to slay the prey whose bounty, whose life, she wants; nay she needs.

It is her desires that she reflects are deserved.

She dreams of a methodical lustful roll.

Sexually capturing her prey in a tomb of woven doom.

She waits.... night in and day out....day in and night out...she enacts seductive interludes.

With time she adds to the weave, ever more complex, tighter still the intrigue.

More desperate become the plans for herself but more-so for her begotten.

However the snare does not ensnare.

She bides her time...time bides her...time too precious to lose.

She senses the loss, the empty web; she considers no thoughts to change the fate.

The lust-filled design so intricate in composition has become an empty tomb of her own.

A tomb which the not-so-hapless prey sees from afar.

The prey his freedom intact is in the place, before the web, they shared a space.

He watches, listens, and waits to see how long before the spider realizes the loss.

The plots, the plans, the complex sexual web all lay in barren deceit.

The prey had seen the spider weave the web, lay the plans, voice it's plots, hear its desperation, listen to the foolishness.

The spider waits on.

She thinks: "Oh! How I did love him!".

Yet she must preserve her species, her offspring is evolution's priority.

It must come at his expense, his lifeblood, regardless of the dearness or the nearness

She holds for the prey that she must have.... if only?

The prey has only sadness for the complex web of the spider's genetic foolishness.

So instead of enjoying the beauty of the world, the true happiness of togetherness and the joys of companionship they grew apart, now distant.

Some webs solely meant to be beautiful in design but empty of purpose.

The prey flits away enjoying each day.

He knows... She pretends to not know that he knows.

Departure and distance, one of sorrow.

Does he miss her...yes, of course?

Will there be a returning...well no...it is the web you know!

≈

SOLO

Love to drive by myself.

A solitary trek.

Alone and free.

No need to talk or entertain.

It's the recluse in me.

Being the hermit alone that I sometimes fear.

Solo driving a wonderful pleasure.

Especially when the final destination captures my attention.

Where a new and exciting adventure await.

Where what to expect is anticipation itself.

What can be more thrilling than a bubbly lady?

One who needs hugging.

More than a hug she deserves.

A kiss of affection, a lift of the spirits, a shot at elation.

Might this task be too much for aged me.

Might like Pandora's box all sorts of vices escape.

Wishing the last to escape are rays of hope.

With wheels on the road.

Wayside flashing by to this tryst I almost fly.

Fly to the hope of elation.

For her, for me, to possibly our eternal damnation.

≈

JESTER

The court of the Klunkers where every member is a Jester and each Jester believes himself King.

Each adorned with garments of silk festooned with colors, stripes and beams of professional radiance.

His robe of regal glitter shows signs of glory, magnificence and splendor.

He wears an ermine sash trimmed with the accomplishments of a golden Aramco Project Management past.

Each Jester possesses inner wear that emit macho energy, enlightened self-confidence and portly commitment.

So boastful is he of his accomplishments, so as to cause, his undies to be chocolate stained.

Each Jester pays homage to all Klunker others.

To them time passages have no tock, no tick and all clocks run backward.

Where yesterday is in the present and the present was once called the future.

Where many dreams of Arabia just happened, or maybe not, at least the Jester thinks they did.

No push, no pull, just the most tenuous touch to time.

Where a warp of time twists back on itself in a place called the Jester's Klunker court.

True to their collective past existence there are no beggars, no users, no leeches, no abusers each Klunker in turn pays his way.

Not so curious each has earned a regal perch by the ethics of hard work.

Now a self-inflicted reincarnation allows each to pursue vaporous dreams which include and exclude going back.

Life of one's youth and careers of pursuit are now left behind to fond and fond-less memories.

War stories abound, not of war, but clashes of a different sort.

Each more glorious with the retelling.

Recanted again and again for the glory and amusement.

Not for the listener but of the re-teller.

Some have squandered a life to energy, some to drink and a bit of debauchery.

Some in the act of doing.

Some still daydreaming that they have - other wishing they hadn't.

Each an entity alike, as they are different.

So what guides the Jester King's star-ship?

One cannot say because they joke and prance to the tune of "I've had my day".

Why question at all a Jester's action?

Especially since the Jester earned the right to be King.

For you see the Jester King is up and doing.

Each pursuing the life's dream - heaven here and heaven there.

The Jester King surely knows his courtly life was accomplished sub-rosa - his Shangri-la.

≈

BONES

A good happy life needs, a wish bone, a backbone and a funny bone.

A wish bone for goals and something to look forward to.

A backbone to work hard and to persevere.

A funny bone for a sense of humor in the face of adversity and a proper outlook on life.

≈

BLUNDER

When things go bad we blame others.

Seldom casting doubt upon self-behavior.

Not our action but that of the moon, sun and stars.

We never are the villain; trickery strikes from behind.

Entropy's chaos, unknown unknowns, plots from evildoers.

All sharing in misfortune's mission.

I but a victim.

Blameless of the blunder.

I promise not to do it again.

≈

CHANGE

I won't change you.

You shan't me.

Loving the other for who they are,

Is perfect you'll see.

≈

"I"

The "I" knows only me and not the other whose body I see.

Yet me, "I" in total do not see.

None but "I" is in my skin, only when I jump out can another pop in.

≈

ROAD SAGE

Life is a drive.

The destination a well lived end.

Shift the transmission without a grind.

First gear is self-reliance.

Responsibility in second.

Conscience found in over-drive.

AVERAGE

In the world of genes it's all inherited stuff.
Your peas are either wrinkled or smooth.

Yet true life is a blend of things.
You are not tall nor a dwarf but somewhere in between.

≈

TEMPERAMENT

Not everyone is kind.
Not many thoughtful or liable to care.
But within any day there is always a chance.

≈

COMMODE

Cyberspace is like a commode.
You crap in it.
Piss all over it standing up.

And then with the flick of a send knob.
A flush, a swirl away.
Poof it is gone.

Don Erdek

MUSINGS

Life is a true miracle in each of us.

Be thankful and gracious to have lived.

Do not fear the deep dark tunnel of the yet to be.

Yet hope there is light.

We shouldn't look for a better time or place.

Appreciate the here and now.

This must be the best there is.

Otherwise, it wouldn't be

If I run they bite my ass.

If I stand still they screw me.

The stroke of nature's clock extracts its toll.

Its movement slow but omnipresent.

To deny its weight is fool's gold.

We have a simplicity of being.

The one and only self.

Each of us our own god

Look nowhere but inward.

Conscious and Conscience are flip sides of the same coin.

It may not be the prime of life.

It may not be a grim stage.

Surely it is a time to itself.

God finds me every day because I look for him.

He is easy to find because I know how to look.

I had no-say so in my creation.

It required the act of two others.

Anything less than perfect is unacceptable.

American culture has steadily become more vulgar.

The earth is round,

Round and sound,

Made for human life to adhere.

Because we choose to believe life is special.

Might it be neither, but just because.

Special enough to cherish each moment.

Wondering is one's life more pushed than pulled?

Now "Faith" can be conjured up while lying (or lie-ing pun intended) on a secluded bench.

It is neither planned nor did fate seek a purpose.

Lying on that hard wooden bench with a prayer rug for a pillow.

More like a ghost emerging from the non-existing ether.

Neither an epiphany nor some sort of musing, merely one person choosing to think.

STORIES

CAFFE MOCHA LADY .117
SLING CAT 119
THE CURIO CABINET AND CURIOSITY 121
CURIOUSITY URGES THE WRITTEN WORD 126
INTIMIDATION 132
MEMORIES OF A RAILROAD 135
A LANTERN GUIDES A RITE OF PASSAGE 137
ON A BENCH 140
OLD FOLK OF TODAY, MY BROTHER GEORGE & I 142
A KLUNKER RENDEZVOUS 143
ARABIAN CRUDE 146
THE SUKS OF OLD AL KHOBAR 146
AL KHOBAR TODAY 148
PICKLES 150
THE GREAT KETCHUP CAPER 152
CRAZY KAZ 155
KAZ 155
TRUST 156
HEARING THE WHOOSH OF A SHOOTING STAR 159
EVOLUTION OF THE SOLAR SYSTEM, SUN & DIRT .163
BILLUMS CREEK 172
A FLORAL EXHALE FOR FAUNA LIFE 179
THE JELLY FISH 184
THE TURTLE 190
ACTION OF A LESSOR GOD 192
THE HUMAN ANATOMY 196
THE WILL TO LIVE 198
CRUISING & FINDING THE FOUNDING FATHERS 206

≈

STORIES

Each day adds another page to our life story.

Not ever a blank one.

Not possible if we but breathe.

There are spectacular ones; others we rather dismiss.

Some full of pride, others burdened with sorrow.

Most mundane but even these are chockfull with the essence of existence.

Of greatest importance is the partly-written page labeled "today".

It is started but yet to be completed.

What it will be is up to thee.

CAFFE MOCHA LADY

We have all visited a Starbucks at one time or another.

To some it's a daily happening.

The visits and the coffees are pleasant enough.

Today Starbucks was different ... or was it the carnal over-cloud in my head?

I had arrived at the coffee house listless and sleepy.

A fitful night plagued with rumpled sheets and ribbons of sensual dreams.

I was not yet sure where dream-sleep end and conscious control arise.

Needing a jolt of Joe to shoo the cobwebs and secure my reverie, unprepared for what happened next.

After placing my order for a Caffe Mocha, I seated myself, relaxed and drifted away.

A Nubian princess appears rich, dark, aromatic and sensually desirable.

The heat of her body emanates through the porcelain cloak which wraps her body.

A feathery white froth adorns her regal brow.

Her body's Arabic aroma glides across my senses.

Her image, her warmth, her smells stir primordial emotions.

She soothes prehistoric urgings.

I sprinkle, no lade, sweet diamond crystals upon her body to enhance her natural charms.

I ask myself, "Have I long last found my one and only true love?"

"Can true love be vicarious?"

"Can true love be compressed into a microcosm of time?"

"Could I be but an amorous bird of prey....only wanting, only waiting; only taking?"

I fawn upon her body.

Should I allow but one second to gaze upon her white feathery froth,

Another minute to breathe her aromatic delights,

Prolong time to feel the warmth of her embrace,

Time without end for all the rest.

Instead I seize the opportunity, for time does not stand still.

I bow my head slowly and softly grasp her porcelain body to lift her essence, her being close to my lips.

I allow her soothing warmth and deep aroma to please my senses.

Her beauty melts my desires.

She is now close to me yet I hesitate to take her.

My hands quiver in delight, my lips purse for pleasure.

I ready myself to take the plunge into the awaking day.

"Sir, are you all right"? The gentle voice of a Starbucks barista breaks my reverie.

"Are you OK? Is your Caffe Mocha prepared to your liking? You have been sitting here for so long with such a strange look on your face that I became concerned. If you don't love your beverage, let me know, we'll always make it right."

"No! No! No! Oh no, young lady, I'm more than all right!

I just happen to be truly loving this very extraordinary cup of enchanting coffee.

It is astonishing how anticipating one small sip can create a morning's delight."

SLING CAT

Did you ever have a toy named "sling cat"?

Probably never did.

But if you were poor then toys like "sling cat" were more happen-chance of nature than buys from Toys-R-Us.

You needed to be poor...very, very poor to know what make-do means.

There are those of us who saw hard times.

We were mere babes during the Great Depression.

Still very young during the Great War years of the Forties.

There was never enough money for toys, not even when birthdays came.

Those were the times when a barrel hoop and a stick were fun and a challenge.

When walking the rails ahead of a train was daring-do.

When rolling down the brook hill was sport and bare-ass-beach the place for summer frolic.

No need for pennies, nickels or dimes when it was cheaper to find something free at most any time.

Now the fantastic toy tale about "sling cat".

Unfortunate it was for that cat, which was neither swift not agile enough, to get out of the way of a truck.

And a big truck at that.

I didn't see it happen but I did see the result.

The cat was splat and flat.

Most every wheel must have done its most to pancake that poor thing between road and tire.

There was little I could do but rescue the poor dead animal from more road and tire abuse.

It was flatter than a Frisbee.

With its tail straight out I grabbed a hold and gave it a fast hard fling.

Away from the road it floppily spun.

Up on a tin roof it landed in full sun.

Well for weeks it lay in full sight as a grim reminder of its plight.

Little I could do since it was up too high.

Until that windy day when a gale and a gust lifted it up and away.

Back down to the ground it sailed, hit once, and light as feather slid away.

It was now just a furry piece of dried-out leather having a tail extended and stiff.

Any gust of wind set it in motion and made it skip.

So I grabbed hold of that extended tail and with the flip of the wrist made it fly.

To my delight it not only spun but made a sharp turn and then a loop-de-loop with every try.

"Sling Cat" became its name; doing loop-de-loops was its game.

For weeks "Sling Cat" was a joy.

Little did that poor cat know that it became my toy.

≈

THE CURIO CABINET AND CURIOSITY

Do you remember the "Curiosity Cabinet" or "Curio Cabinet"? In by-gone decades, it was common in many homes.

Those glass-fronted cabinets contained all sorts of mementos, trophies, postcards, perfume bottles, cameos, glass figurines, crystals, porcelain dolls and so many blue or silk ribbons. Each object was a fascination to itself and held an unexplained attraction and tokens of remembrance. They were curiously glittering treasures from places traveled and prizes or trophies won. Each item had a story or a mystery to itself...a curiosity saved.

The "Curio Cabinet" was the family's own little museum.

It guarded family treasures that were often passed down from mother to daughter.

Each of these trinkets was able to tap into fountains of emotions.

Many recreated passionate feelings of happy times and joyous celebrations.

And some found the tender feelings of sentiment.

These were laden with heavy sorrows about an ancestor whose lasting memento evokes a tearful remembrance.

All of these curious little items recreating curiosity of some by-gone time… curiosity now saved.

Children peered into the "Curio Cabinet" with noses pressed close to the glass.

Hands were kept at the sides knowing touching was not allowed.

They were encouraged to ask questions.
Stories of old were then retold most often and mainly for the pleasure of the storyteller.

We all know that children are curious simply because they have so much to learn and everything to them is new.

They are driven by the want to know and the need to learn.

They ask so many questions.

They ask "why" to the exasperation of a parent that often challenges the patience of a saint.

They seek answers and are at life's inquisitive maximum of curiosity.

With age, curiosity wanes.

Inquisitiveness is replaced with an attitude of indifference and the smugness of being all-knowing.

An attitude which does not require any further questions to be asked; or knowledge needed for a life to be lived day to day.

Then comes old age when the body weakens and becomes worn from long use.

As we grow older we tend to become less active.

We rely on what we have already learned to see us through the rest of the journey.

One's life become easily drained of color, interest, and pleasure.

Our minds, they atrophy too; but not from overuse but instead from little use.

Curiosity has succumbed to benign neglect.

While barely noticing it, you have become a little duller...a little dimmer.

So what is this thing we call curiosity?

If we were asked to name the basic human drives we would answer food, shelter and sex.

However I would add a fourth drive...pure curiosity.

Curiosity can be unruly...matter of fact, downright nosy.

Yet, it is a most valuable asset of man's inquiring mind.

In the simplest of terms it is the want to know.

It is that hunger to learn, to question, and ultimately to create.

That drive to make sense of the world is in large part a universal characteristic of any human being.

That is of any human that chooses to know and not merely to follow.

It is essential to an exploring mind.

Curiosity taunts us to examine and explain our world.

It challenges us to pursue the universe as an inspiring, fascinating place.

Curiosity and its dear mate "awareness" have, I am sure, been implanted in us by our Creator.

Yet, so strange it is, that humanity's oldest stories about curiosity are cautionary if not down-right negative.

The oldest being that of Adam and Eve and the apple from the tree of knowledge

Or take the many sources of troubles released when out of curiosity Pandora opened the box.

Or the impertinence of Icarus whose yearn and curiosity to fly with waxen wings were melted by Lord Sun.

Is the moral that if the curious be too brazen, go too far, plunge too deep, they then tempt the hand of Fate?

Religions do not encourage curiosity lest it trifles with faith.

They are all parochial with appeals to the heart and directives to the mind to "be not" curious.

So basic to religion is to believe...do not question..."be not" curious of creation.

But ...curiosity is cool!

Curiosity is a life force.

Curiosity is about oneself.

Curiosity is about the cosmos.

Curiosity is about feelings and the thoughts of others.

Curiosity is absolutely vital to a happy and well lived life.

In the simplest of terms, curiosity is the need to know.

It is the tendency to see and enjoy the world about.

It is the persistence to look for and hunger for novelty.

It is the realization that the most interesting things are those things that are outside of us.

It is the wanting to know of the thoughts and feelings of other people but distinct from gossip or prurience.

The true beauty of curiosity is the learning of apparent useless stuff that takes us beyond our petty selves.

We may need oxygen, sunshine, food and shelter to survive but we need knowledge to thrive.

In today's age of plenty we are no longer burdened by the many basic duties of survival.

We now have so much time to relax and learn.

We die inside if human curiosity isn't fed.

It reminds us that we need to continue to be a part of that far greater project.

Curiosity is a universal trait of mankind, it is contagious but... alas...so is in-curiosity!

So ask questions, seek answers.

Get curious, take little for granted.

And lest you forget, go find and put another memento into the "Curio Cabinet."

≈

CURIOUSITY URGES THE WRITTEN WORD

Humans are born with curiosity.

A desire to comprehend the world we entered.

Curiosity leads to awareness.

Awareness that nature is the greatest mystery.

A mystery that expands from the opening of eyes to the world and the universe beyond.

And even more to the mysteries of the inner self.

It is the search for self.

That entity which breathes and thinks and gathers it all in.

The search for knowledge that is hastened on by curiosity.

Books fill exactly that curiosity search.

They are a great source of feed for a curious appetite.

Become a great receptacle for storage of so many things.

Books hold the curio, the magic, the mystery in the printed word.

They develop patches of knowledge that can stitch together and tailor our own little universe into one fine, silken, golden, magnificent garment.

Or possibly, the playground for a curious mind to find a favorite ride to the real or fantasy.

Books are a library of knowledge and contain the learning and curiosity of others all bound neatly on paper.

So grateful should we be that all those of wisdom who lived before us are at our disposal in books.

Sir Isaac Newton, Einstein, Matthew, Mark, Luke, John and the billions of ordinary men and women who came before.

All who preceded us were confined to an intellectual universe tiny compared to our own of today.

They now sit waiting for us to uncover the curiosity in their life which today handily and boldly is available to us as printed words.

Not only is there more knowledge today, but access to it is phenomenal.

We know of DNA, genetic science, black holes, modern materials, plastics, airplanes and of course computers and electronics.

So much there is to learn, so much to know, if we give but time enough to curiosity.

Careful here...computers have an astounding amount of data but no curiosity!

The same curiosity should be applied to artful or cultural curiosity.

It is the desire to know Michelangelo, Leonardo da Vinci, and even the Beatles and Elvis.

Is it not really great that we have lived after these individuals and not before?

At the risk of being boring allow me this chance to pontificate.

We may grow old and tremble in our anatomy,

We may lie awake at night waiting for sleep to come,

We may lose our one and only love,

We may see the world about us devastated by terrorism and religious fanatics,

Never-the-less, we are living in an age where we can learn so much...add so much to our self.

Maybe, even possibly, to make some little thing better.

Today we can know how the world's tail wags and what wags it.

Curiosity is a therapeutics thing.

No matter what your age, curiosity is the thing for you.

Look at how many things and how much there is yet to learn?

Curiosity can keep your mind active and induce that thinking thing.

Curiosity is an exercise for the brain … to keep it in working condition.

We can stay aware of time, of what is happening at the moment, of the world around us if we be but curious.

Curiosity requires an active brain.

Anyone who chooses to exercise the brain and activate its powers of observation will learn something new each day.

If one becomes tired of learning; one becomes tired of life.

You do not tire if you keep your curiosity alive.

No matter how old one get, we think ourselves young in mind and still vital in spirit.

Are we fooling ourselves?

Maybe not so much!

The body may become old and feeble but it seems so easy to remain enthusiastic in one's mind.

Just let some one thing pique our interest and we become a whole new person.

We can amaze ourselves with how vital and vigorous a person we can be.

Curiosity can be tough to justify at any one moment.

It diverts us from our all too important tasks of naps, idleness, TV, and computer games.

Curiosity can be hard work.

We never know where it will take us.

But we have a choice, especially in later years when we have so much leisure time.

We can decide to explore the world of knowledge that is easier to access than ever before.

Or we can turn our faces from the beauty and the mystery of this one and only existence.

Throughout history, in times of crisis and disaster, we have looked to the future.

If not with the confidence of youth, at least with the hopes of old age.

The messiah will come.

The heathens will be converted.

An Aldous Huxley "Brave New World" will be ushered in.

So what's there to be curious about?

Curious to smell new smells, taste different food, glide one's mind or hand over an odd surface.

Or touch another heart with a smile.

Peer where your eyes never looked before.

Question a belief...something you have accepted all your life without question.

Bite the apple from the tree of knowledge...what now is there to lose?

Question a preacher …pursue a new subject...be curious of a different country, city, or state.

Question a custom…what is an Eskimo's life like?

Why do we have two eyes and not three or more?

Why five fingers, five toes, two legs and two arms?

Just what is gravity?

Why does time go in one direction only...always older?

What is space...and what is there between things that we call space...might it actually be something?

How about Electromagnetism? Our modern life is built upon use of this force.

There is electricity, radio, TV, telephone, computers, I-pad, I-phone.

How about earth's magnetism, black holes, big bang, and the Higgs boson?

Sun's solar rays are photons which are both a wave and a particle at the same time ...how can that be?

Per chance, is ones curiosity a measure of one's life...a gauge of life's worth and vitality?

And by the way what's for dinner?

So ask questions.

Seek answers.

Take little for granted.

Find and put another memento into the "Curio Cabinet".

≈

Don Erdek

INTIMIDATION

Have you ever been intimidated by a plant?

It can happen.

It all started at a local Texas ranch and feed store where a few seed packets lay next to the cash register. Bird House Gourds was printed on the label. No other information was available on how, when, or where to plant. For a dollar what's to lose. How difficult could that be?

It was a simple enough beginning. I saw no warning sign from a small packet of two dozen or so dried seeds. I decided to give it try. Who would or could anticipate nature's auspicious might that was set to be released? Certainly not me!

It was already late June. Too late to be planting seeds in East Texas with the very hot and dry months of July and August just a week or so away - I did it anyway. Luckily, I had a nice remote plot of about 40 feet by 60 feet at the back end of my 73-acre lower pasture. (I may not be telling this story had I chosen a site closer to the ranch house.) I was experimenting with growing fruit trees, so I had built an eight-foot-high steel game wire and post fence around the small fruit trees to protect them from the deer and grazing cattle. I had kept the enclosed area nicely roto-tilled so it was an easy chore to mound up some loose dirt into a few hills and drop 3 or 4 gourd seeds in each.

Well July and August of 2002 were as hot as expected, but unexpected, were the periodic rains that precluded any drought. The seeds quickly sent up 2-inch-high shoots and within 2 weeks vines started creeping out in all directions from each mound of dirt. Like the tentacles from an octopus, the fences and trees were being used for climbing skyward. The small fruit trees were besieged. The spiral tentacles of the gourd plants wound like toy Slinkies around trunks and limbs. From the beginning, I periodically freed the trees from the murderous plant's choking grasp. But each following day they were back, more tenacious, more onerous then before. I coaxed the persistent vines toward the eight-foot-high game fence believing that was a controlling climb. The vines responded with glee and rapture, climbing almost overnight. Within weeks the fences were inundated and trees totally engulfed. All were submerged by the spirals of ten thousand miniature boa constrictors.

I gave up and got out of the way of the demon plants. I would start to enter the area, but immediately felt intimidated and would quickly back out of the fenced area in disbelief to what was happening. The plants were in control. A solid carpet of vines and huge saucer shaped leaves two-foot-deep covered the entire fenced in area. There was no longer open ground. No place to step, I couldn't believe what I was seeing - what the plants were doing. They were metastasizing at an alarming rate.

The plants slithered up and over the perimeter fence, over the entrance gate, sealing it shut. I stopped trying to enter the area. Gourd heads emerged everywhere, rising up like ugly green spheres emerging from a green carpet grave. The fences were totally engulfed, now hidden in clinging vines and huge spooky green leaves, hiding how it was possible for the plants to continue remaining erect. The fences began sagging from the vines and the huge pendant gourds - too many to count. The trees, they were on their own. Things had become scary.

After dark it was a no-go area.

By August the steel fences could no longer stand the strain and they began to lean and sag. Within weeks the steel posts were bending over to meet the ground. The gourds were huge and there were so many - everywhere. I worried about what was being created.

October came with little let-up to the massive growth; there was no break in the canopy of green. The vines had now metastasized in some places to twenty feet beyond what once was a fenced enclosure. What was vine and what was serpent was indistinguishable. For sure it was nature's cloak to ensure the security of one and the other. In turn, nature's camouflage intimidated even the purported most intelligent animal on the planet. Finally by the middle of October some of the leaves and vines began to dry. But even at that, it was only with stealth that I would enter the area to retrieve the first gourds whose stems turned brown.

By the first of November I entered with enough confidence that I no longer preplanned an escape route. By the end of November all leaves and vines had withered away. All totaled I harvested 573 gourds from the plot. Now only mangled fences remain as an eerie tattletale of a tiny seed packet that spawned demon plants.

Alas, the saga does not end here. Its ominous existence continued elsewhere. I now have these 573 gourds hanging from the rafters in the attic section of my garage. As you might know the gourds, they each have their own almost grotesque and misshaped identity and each dry in a different way. When drying , the exterior of some of the gourds harden and splay colors like the skin of a 4000 year old mummy, while others for no apparent reason, become covered with aging liver spots, or white cottony mold, or ugly black slimy soot, or a combination of all of these. All normal, so I've been told, but not a pretty sight.

Well do you have any idea what it's like to enter a dimly lit attic, where above your head, hanging from the rafters are hundreds of pendulant, misshapen, mold and soot covered objects hanging in patient silence. It's like Dracula's cave or a head-hunters treasure trove. Picture it as something out of a Hollywood horror film where demon arises in new form in another location to haunt once more.

Now, I'm told that it may take up to a year for these gourds to dry. So when I again must enter their zone, I tie a rope around my waist and leave instructions to pull me out if I don't emerge in five minutes.

I tell this tale as I saw it happen. Not a demon plant you say. Well I checked with two other gourd growers in the area and one relates limited success with good vines but only 3 gourds. The other said "a dismal failure, everything rotted". As for a picture of me in my garden, all I can say is "No way!", all my pictures were taken from a distance.

≈

MEMORIES OF A RAILROAD

Something neat about old trains.

Even abandoned railroad tracks were compelling.

Many of us in our youth walked the rails to prove balance.

Who lasted longer or went faster further without falling off became the tight-rail champ of the track.

Then there was railroad roulette...climbing up and over those huge boxcars to boxcar couplers of a stopped train.

More daring still, crawling under the massive undercarriage of a tanker and lingering there longer than any other while daring the train to start to move.

Who hasn't rode a slow-moving train or hopped on a train just as it started to move and rode it as it picked up speed.

Daring your friends as to who will be the last to jump off.

Laying your ear close to a rail to hear if a far-off train is coming your way. Or putting pennies on the rails in front of an on-coming speeding train and then looking to find the flattened copper.

Who didn't consider the hobo, a man to admire as a man of adventure living a carefree life unencumbered by the need to work?

And didn't we all say "crap" when they retired the caboose.

The faded red caboose was a national railroad treasure with the old guy standing on the back waving goodbye or the red lanterns fading as the train move away at night.

Leaving you to wonder where the train was going, who was on board, what was its cargo and why can't you be on it.

I think it's the yearning to see the world.

It's that spark, that desire, to be a tumbleweed, to travel and witness firsthand Earth's wonders.

When I was in my late teens I had a curfew to be home by midnight.

Often it was well after curfew that I was on my way home and sure to wake Mom.

Well we lived but a half block from the railroad tracks.

I knew that every night at 2AM a fast-moving freight came by so I would wait until it arrived.

Then I would zoom into the drive, into the house, and up the stairs as it rumbled by.

The next morning Mom would always ask what time I got in and my answer was "early"...no lie there!

The funny part of this story is that one night as I raced home because it was almost time for the 2AM freight to arrive that lo and behold there was my younger brother in his car waiting in my spot for the same noisy train's arrival.

We both had a laugh that long-ago early morning as we zoomed up the stairs together with the noise of the train in the background.

Yep....railroads and trains have always captured my interest.

Who hasn't stood on and looked down an empty track without having the desire to go somewhere...anywhere?

And that forlorn train whistle so far away in the middle of the night waking you just enough that you wonder in sleepiness that someone and his train is going somewhere right now as you sleep.

I think it's the yearning to see the world.

It's that spark, that desire, to be a tumbleweed, to travel and witness firsthand Earth's wonders.

≈

A LANTERN GUIDES A RITE OF PASSAGE

It was a long time ago for I am an old man now.

My mind's eye can still see the Coleman lantern's orange-white light sitting in the middle of an oversized table.

Huddled around and mesmerized by the lamp's glow are six cocoon-like figures.

Six young boy scouts sit Indian style atop a rough-hued table, each drawing strength from the nearness, seeking composure, from the comradery and a lantern.

Only the oval of faces peered out from sleeping bag encased bodies reveal the existence of life.

The lantern's steady light and soft energy their eyes only focus.

That long-ago January night was the first of three wilderness tests to be passed, alone without adult supervision, to enter a new order of scouting, the Sons of Hiawatha.

The day passed bitter cold, the requirements to hike, track, cook outdoors, and find a specific camp location were successfully done.

Constructing a log bridge across a swollen waterway the only real challenge.

Sub-zero daytime temperatures plunged lower as night approached and the wind's howl and moan was in lockstep with the night's dark-fall.

The day's ten-mile trek into the mountains and through a craggy gorge ended at this remote Boy Scout nature lodge which normally is used only for summer excursions.

The lodge was not reached until dusk.

The interior of the lodge provided adequate shelter even with the many strong drafts entering from between the unsealed logs.

Upon arrival the scouts each selected and settled in on the several bunk beds that were built along a far wall.

But almost in unison they abandoned the bunks for that wooden table.

Although the cabin was shelter from the howling wind and bitter cold it created its own form of apprehension.

On the shelves were animal skulls surrounded by an array of bare bleached white bones, there were countless formaldehyde filled jars with rattlesnakes, salamanders, spiders and tadpoles floating grotesquely within, a mounted raccoon greedily grabbing for something in the open air, a bobcat silently snarled showing a full mouth of sharp teeth, a she wolf protecting her pups, but most ominous was that five-foot wing-spanned vulture with beady red piercing eyes swooping down from the ceiling right above the door to the outside.

The first hour of that evening they discussed their tasks and shared an elation in being alone, in control, and pride in their accomplishments.

However not one of the boys was eager to leave the group and go to bed.

None admitted to the slow creep of anxiety.

Anxiety created by the solitude and remoteness of the location heightened by the frigid-cold outside and wailing wind.

Anxiety soon turned to fear of those many hideous wide-open eyes peering intently from the bottles, from the ghastly and ghostly animals stationed at each corner of the room and especially from the vulture hanging just above their heads guarding the exit door.

So they had sought companionship and gathered around that central table.

Uneasy talk became a silence as slowly, one but one, each abandoned the benches to climb up on the table and be closer to the glow and succor of the lantern.

The day's youthful elation had become a creeping anxiety which then overcame them with fears of the night.

The sentinel lantern kept watch over the silence, its glow softened the fears, finally dimming the lids into drowsy sleep.

And when morning dawned none could recall how long the orange glow continued.

Each knew it lasted longer than they did and had become the guide and light to cross that rite of passage.

≈

Don Erdek

ON A BENCH

Today was a fine day to sit on a bench.

I took the dog for a walk and went to the park.

Took off her leash and let her run.

On a bench under a not too tall oak tree I let my aging frame gently settle down.

Tilted my head back and took a skyward gaze.

Past the branches, through the leaves, then just relaxed and let that which is me also unleash.

The sky a dome of soothing softening blue capping the oasis we call Earth.

North was there just ahead and West was to my left so the sun said.

The summer breeze was warm and as it slipped past my left ear it felt so soft and light.

So gentle with its invisible touch it makes its presence known like only air can stroke and rub.

So little attention we pay to air.

We take for granted that it has always been here.

Made for us on this planet earth; made to create the blue in the sky.

Made for us to breathe, to smell, for its oxygen to make our blood sound.

Or do we have that not quite right.

Might it be we who from elsewhere or nowhere found our place with air above and dirt below.

Might it be Nature with all its might and with endless time make our matter right.

To many, it is attributed to the hand of a creator.

But does not nature have a hand in everything created, in everything human?

So might Nature and the Creator be one and the same?

I, myself, see no reason to separate that glory, that magnificence, that omnipotence.

At this moment I am glad and relaxed with what there is

To expand a moment in time and reflect on a life.

An existence personal to me.

Shared with no one and everyone at the same time.

All of us, now, before, and those to come after, share the legend and magnificence of humankind.

Shared even with my pooch as I glance to see her off in the distance sniffing the grass.

So intense is she to find someone else's splendid sensual natural pee

These moments in time are glorious and real.

Elegant and basic each with its own appeal.

Whether a feel of the air or a sniff of the scented grass.

A moment of time ... a fine day to sit on a bench.

Don Erdek

OLD FOLK OF TODAY - MY BROTHER GEORGE AND I

My brother George and I, and some other old folk of today, are deeply worried about what is happening.

We have grown old but as can be expected, always hoping for a few more good years.

We think about being loved but yet we are not so loved as to be listened to.

After all that's all we have left - the years gone by, the experience, the knowledge that comes with age.

So try to put yourself in our old shoes and bodies.

We are like a worn-out vehicle with an experienced driver behind the wheel.

Once we were a new car of life with an inexperienced driver.

We zoomed fast covering a lot of unexplored ground, building roads and things of wonder from imagination.

We drove well, I do believe even the youth of today would agree.

We moved it forward at a rapid pace, year after year, few pit stops if any at all.

We slowed for bumps in the road but dawdled not and with eagerness made-up for lost time.

Advancing on all fronts which was truly a moving forward in substance and not merely rhetoric.

Today we have inexperienced youthful drivers bemoaning and blaming the road we paved.

Is really the path of our years not the guide, not nearly enough to suit the deserving or to provide for the entitled?

So let me say!

We are now like those old tires on life's vehicle.

An old tire feels the rocks and bumps so much harder, ever sharper.

The pressures of economy so much more felt on the side walls of our bodies.

The treads of life worn smooth by the abrasion of toil.

Our ribs of steel weakened by the roughness of the miles.

The valves of the heart so close to not being able to contain the pressure.

The rubber, the polymer, the fabric of what we once were, being weakened by not being rotated to spare.

Worse still!

Much worse!

We are being declared Klunkers to life.

≈

A KLUNKER RENDEZVOUS

Klunkers gather to the scribe's direction.

Like the spokes of a Texas wheel they converge.

At just before high noon at a house of repast they each listen a lot but talk so much more.

Around a table with four chairs bare the Klunker Rendezvous convenes.

A noisy unrestrained carouse with no pattern, no venue.

A string of unstoppable stories, opinions and answers.

A jejune of life, morals, lies, half-truths and their reflections.

All clacking, clamoring and lip-chattering in unison.

Each Klunker believes himself blessed.

Each with age and wisdom, a frail body at best.

Each Klunker pays homage to the others by listening to stories of old Aramco, often being retold.

Where time passages have no tock, no tick, and the clock runs backward.

Where yesterday is in the present and the present is what was their future.

Where many dreams just happen.

No push, no pull just a time warp to fall into.

This is the space called the Klunker Rendezvous.

True to their past existence there are no beggars, no users, no leeches and in time each takes a turn.

Not so curious that each has earned a regal perch by the ethics of diligent hard work.

The life of one's youth, long hours and a career of pursuit are now behind them with fond and fond-less memories.

War stories and past antics abound.

Each more glorious and exaggerated at another retelling.

Recanted again and again for the glory and amusement of not the listener but of the re-teller.

Some are still in the act of doing.

And yet all are still dreaming, still pursuing.

Each an entity so alike as they are so different.

So what guides the Klunker Starship?

What nebulous desires consume their waning living moments?

The space ahead much shorter than that already traversed.

The fact of the matter lies in the jokes and dancing to the tune of "I cannot say".

All of this begs another question of "Why question at all a Klunker's talk?"

Hasn't each earned a Klunker's right to be free and not junk of an Obama decree.

A tie that binds is hard to detect perhaps it be nothing more than a fine silken weave of mutual respect.

All Klunkers know that each Rendezvous shows his sub-rosa - his Shangri-la.

Always a Klunker is up and doing.

Each pursuing just "a little bit of heaven" in the glory of yesteryear.

Simple to see that a Klunker Rendezvous is host and forum to a Klunker's Aramco reverie.

ARABIAN CRUDE

The Americans were here!

The Americans were here!

They found the crude.

They produced the crude.

They shipped the crude.

They bought the crude.

The King got the gold.

The Americans are gone.

The Saudis own it all.

It will run for 200 years.

≈

THE SUKS OF OLD AL KHOBAR

The sounds, the sights, the smells of old Khobar.

'Twenty rial', 'twenty rial', 'Come see my shop...Welcome – Ahalen Wasalla'.

The tailor shop, the gold merchant, frame a picture.

Cover the nose with a hand when passing those no lid containers.

Black veils and Abiya to hide the skin.

Blonde curls expose the foreign.

Thirteen bracelets a must for the perfect women.

Silver will do, but surely you know it is gold that creates the sweetest glow.

Into the Indian shop at first prayer call.

Miniature silk prayer rugs, fine coasters used best to sponge the spill of siddiqi.

Search for a unique Khanjak, that crescent shape hip dagger of Arabian renown.

Check prices of brass coffee pots, compare to those of Tex.

That super hawker who makes Dhahran and Abqaiq rounds.

Claiming his accent is God-given.

Didn't know Travis or Austin ever left Texas.

Adan is over, doors reopen, back into the street, avoiding the dirty mangy cat asleep by the door.

Repair a broken belt, get a new buckle, a new pair of silver earrings, check out that new vendor only because.

For sure a shawarma on hot khubza bread.

Watching first the thin slices of meat fall away along with the grease and the heat.

Shoo away a fly to get that first bite.

Pepsi to drink, no such thing here as Coke.

The bustle, the hustle, a dodge and a weave snaking around the Thobs on the walk.

Abiyas and Gutras causing a spider-like dance along a craggy sidewalk.

Into the Tariq, across a dark alley, yielding to the Toyota that you know won't stop.

Notice the old guys in a hookah place, lounging around a small tea table exchanging some tale.

The sweet smell of hashish floating in the air.

Getting directions that include the mosque, the road to Dhahran, Eve's jewelry or King Khalid main street.

Can't get lost but finding a parking place to have hidden the Aramco vehicle a must do first task.

A few right turns, a couple of go-around, the ladies still looking, the guys bored out of their skulls.

Deciding to go home knowing the trip left things undone, "Yimkin bukara" for sure "Inshalla".

≈

AL KHOBAR TODAY

Present day Suqs of Al Khobar are not the same.

So very different from Aramco's American days.

Action has departed this once active place.

Modern life has passed it by.
Things built around and nearby have changed the tempo.
Zoom, zoom, vast number of cars pass by, scoot around.

Where they go - not to stop.
At least not to park, not to shop.
Not here their destination.

Quiet has descended.
People-less alleys.
Darkened and abandoned shops.

It still exists.
It still is there.
Not much of an atmosphere.

Things have changed, certainly not for the better.
Social life has left for elsewhere.
What remains is but a lifeless whisper of the past.

Business and enterprise is a sky-line away.

Built around leaving the Suqs to decay.

Abandoning the hub to a hallow existence.

Not much happening, nobody here.

The streets are bare, once a bustle now a bust.

What glittered with gold is now dusty and old.

Joy and excitement has abandoned this once exciting place.

Now Eve's is still there.

As is King Khalid street.

The Silver Museum has lights on.

The sidewalks are shabbier, the alleys dimmer.

If cracks could have cracks and rubble can become rubblier, then it is here still.

Smells the same, phew is phew, whether old or new.

No hustle, no bustle.

The Americans have left.

≈

PICKLES

Somebody has been in my pickle jar.

It seems not too long ago that it was a chore to get that first pickle out of the pickle jar.

It was a marvel how they managed to get that last pickle pushed so tightly in.

One needed a fork to stab and pry to get that first pickle loose and up and out.

But no more.

Now pickles are poorly packed.

They now float around in the jar like a pod of green whales in the open sea.

Ok, so the price of pickles has not been increased.

But paying the same price for less pickles has turned into less bang for the buck.

Or in this case less pickle packing.

I've noticed the same less bang for the buck phenomenon elsewhere.

Say candy bar sizes or restaurant portions.

So now I wonder how many less pickles in a pickle jar another pickle jar can make.

Or how do they price polish pickles from picker to packer so price is practically packed.

Anyhow polish pickles pleases me to have a powerful pucker no matter what price the pickle packer picks.

≈

Don Erdek

THE GREAT KETCHUP CAPER

There is a sneak assault by the food industry on another sacred tradition.

They beset us with a fluid attack upon our pickle jars with pickles unpacked.

Now our Ketchup bottles they find to defile.

Ketchup indeed was a rich, thick paste.

A culinary delight for every taste.

The flavor, the tang, a thickness to last

It's inability to flow and hold on to that fry gave time for the savor.

We all remember how hard it was to get Ketchup to flow.

That new bottle, that first dollop just wouldn't come out.

Try as we may it stay stuck in the spout.

Everyone swore on their own special trick to get that first lick out.

Everyone advised everyone else on sure success to master Ketchup viscosity that gave us a test.

Everyone watched everyone else to see what worked.... how to get out that first squirt.

A 45-degree tilt of the bottle and infinite patience.

Five swift raps with the heal of the palm on the butt of the bottle is sure to un-throttle.

The handle of a spoon stuck down its neck got a messy spoon and not much else.

Pushed to frustration we often abandoned the Ketchup and reach for the mustard.

But no longer!

Someone has messed with the Ketchup.

Diluted I suspect to increase the profit.

To ease the flow at the expense of your pocket.

Now that first squirt from the bottle erupts.

Across the burger, the plate, and the table.

A diarrhea red liquid of something that's certainly ain't Ketchup.

Who is to clean this red watery mess and how to get it off of my chest?

The real Ketchup is still in the bottle.

What came out I haven't a clue but its fluid and now running off the table and on to my shoe.

My French fries are soggy and limp; the burger, the bun now soaked with the stuff.

It now looks so bad it ain't fit to eat so call over the dog it's his treat.

Political correctness, environmental concern, economy considered at every turn.

Shake the Ketchup vigorously before you pour this will help to spread the wealth.

Big government, Health Care and Latino votes are the priority and not your taste.

Clever producers hide the caper by turning the bottle upside down.

Do your share it's not a chore.... just shut up and pour.

Don Erdek

CRAZY KAZ

Back in New Jersey many, many, years ago in my youth I had a group of friends that were young and a bit crazy. But one stood out from the rest and that was Crazy Kaz. We were now all out of high school and yet to get serious about life. Most of us had just taken our first jobs mostly as laborers.

Now we would gather each evening some place downtown to kill time. Most of the times it was in Dolly Madison's. It was an ice cream parlor and a great gathering place to start the evening's nonsense of youth. Old enough to drive, still too young to drink legally, but always looking to find a way.

Now Crazy Kaz had gotten his first job in a pickle factory. New Jersey is the garden state and known for good produce and good small canning cucumbers. The pickle factory was known to hire local youth and give them a head start at better than minimum wage.

Soon after Kaz got the job he told the gathering of friends that he has an urge to put his thing in the pickle cutter. We all knew Kaz to be crazy but this was going a bit far so we told him not to do any of his typical crazy stuff if he wants to keep that good paying job.

Well almost every evening he told us guys that the urge to put his thing in the pickle cutter is still with him. Finally one evening he told the guys that he got fired from the job because he found a way to put his thing in the pickle cutter. We all immediately asked him if he was ok and not hurt.

He said yeah he was ok but he felt bad for the pickle cutter.

What!!!!!! ....why do you feel sorry for the pickle cutter?

He grinned and said well she got fired too.

≈

KAZ

My friend of many years.

I love you, Man!

Knew you would be there whenever I dropped by.

No schedule, no plan.

No reason to explain.

Always a welcome.

A chance to go back to Manville before.

We were young again whenever we met.

Can't ever recall a disagree.

Never a crossing of swords ⚔□.

How can that be!

Now, years later we are still fine friends.

So many years of life to share.

Not together nor ever in spirit apart.

A friend in mind never departs.

≈

TRUST

My recent trip from Fort Myers/Estero, Florida to Lufkin, Texas was a 1200-mile road jaunt of "TRUST." Maybe it's only me but I feel I'm going uphill/downhill or sideways on long road trips. Take for instance this trip which needed but three main interstates and only two 90 degree turns to complete.

Starting at Fort Myers/Estero I got on I-75 and then it's a straight shot due North for 300 miles to Lake City and I-10. Take a 90-degree left turn and then 800 miles due West on I-10 to Beaumont, Texas. Another 90 degree turn but this time to the right on I-69 due North for 100 miles puts me smack dab into the heart of Lufkin.

When driving North I truly feel I'm going up-hill. When driving west I feel I'm going sideways and against a current flowing East. I wonder if this is because North points up as the Earth revolves around the Sun? And when going west it seems to be going against the Earth's rotation on its axis? Does anyone have these same feelings and does it mean anything? Should we "TRUST" these feelings?

And then there is a "TRUST" in whoever is driving the car. Since my wife doesn't "TRUST" my driving she insists on the majority of wheel time (Don't throw this Brer Rabbit into that non-drive briar patch!!!!) Hell, I don't like driving anyways and the road sounds and tire noise soothes my road naps.

But when she does let me drive, she acts and reacts as though the steering wheel is still in front of her. Turn here...Get in the other lane...Your driving too fast...Too slow...Watch that car on the left... etc. And that passenger side floor mat take's one hellava brake foot pounding.

But you see I do "TRUST" her driving. She is a very careful driver who has an absolute unwavering self-requirement to obey all speed limit signs. That is despite the zoom-zoom of other drivers left and right speeding past her as though she were driving backward.

But even she has her own form of road rage. I call it "decibel screaming". I don't know how many times I've been awoken from my slumber by "ASSHOLE," "DUMBSHIT," and "friggen women or old man." She yells this so loud that I have cauliflower ears from the percussion. I've tried to explain to her (nicely of-course) that all those other drivers "really" can't hear her. But this old man passenger might just crap his pants from the sonic shock wave. Her defense to me is that those yells may upset me but it sure does make her feel better.

At one stage of the trip somewhere between Mobile, Alabama and Biloxi, Mississippi my mind wandered back to three old guys gathering that discussed the topic of "TRUST". It was not that long ago that these three friends gathered under the wide-open spaces of the Texas sky. They were alone and away from the women folk and sitting somewhere along the southern Texas coast about where Rockport kisses-off Mustang Island. More specific they were drinking beer in a 30-foot RV and bullshitting as old angry white men often do. They had already planned a sortie of necessity across a foot bridge into Mexico and to the border town Reynosa for the next day. But today, the out-of-the-blue topic of "TRUST" arose. It was a very general, ill-defined question that each responded with a one-word one-number answer. Now the question was "Just how much do you "TRUST" your fellow man to do the right thing in any given situation"? Let me further clarify that these three guys are basically cut from the same political, social, economic type of cloth. One was a Down-Easterner, another a Jersey-boy, and the other a New Mexico Mescalero. Same cloth...yeah...Right... FAR RIGHT.

When answering the question the Jersey-Boy said ... about 53%. The New Mexico Mescalero said...maybe 26 to 27%. The Down-Easterner frowned and remarked...no more than 3%. Well I'm not sure what to make of this or what conclusions we can take away other than..."Why such a variance?". And if these numbers are anywhere near correct we really don't trust many people very often.

Actually those three friends fell silent, dropped the subject and never returned to it again.

So what does that story have to do with "TRUST" on that Fort Myers/Estero to Lufkin trip? Well quite a lot!!!!.and quite an enigma. For you realize that when you are sitting in a car going 70-75 miles per hour your "TRUST" level is peaking at 99.9999%.

First of all is, the driver, and it doesn't matter whether you are driving or not. Just consider the 4000-pound vehicle you are in going at 70 MPH. We can calculate the energy, the inertia and the thrust but let's just say it's a "LOTS-Of." You can imagine what may happen if that "LOTS-Of" meets dead-on with a Jersey wall or a concrete bridge abutment. "LOTS OF TRUST" here that the driver won't let that happen.

Then there are those other drivers especially those in 18 wheelers careening down the highway. And your car gets sandwiched in the middle lane of a three-lane highway and all going 70 MPH plus. A 50 ton plus behemoth to the right and a tanker with a skull sticker warning FLAMMABLE on your left. What is the mass inertia here? And what's the "TRUST" level at this time or do we just pucker our ass and let it grab the seat?

And those semi drivers, how long have they been behind the

wheel? How much caffeine, 5-hour energy shots, hip-hop pills have they taken? Got to scare the be-jesuss out of you if you bothered to think about it.

Then when, you finally get to I-69 it becomes a two-lane highway with a 75 MPH speed limit. So that 3/4-ton pick-up coming at you is closing at a combined rate of 150 MPH and will be passing within maybe 6 or 8 feet between? Is that pick-up driver drunk or high? Texting? An imbecile? A novice? On the cell phone? Or about to nod off and cross the center line? Don't even think front wheel blow-out.

So what's the point here? Is there any moral?

We trust other humans to do the right thing maybe 3% or even 53 % of the time. But we enshroud ourselves with a mechanical tin shell and all of a sudden our trust becomes 99.999%. Have we lulled ourselves into a state of complacency out of necessity?

GO FIGURE!

≈

HEARING THE WHOOSH OF A SHOOTING STAR

It is midnight on a starry, starry night deep in the heart of Texas. I'm on the upper deck of the ranch house sited smack in the middle of seventy-three acres of my ranch I call - Dande. My eyes adjust to the darkness. My senses slide open trying to grasp the awe of the night sky My limited understanding of this whole creation demanding an explanation, captivating my attention.

My mind unfreezes, opens wide searching for some understanding. I start to wonder about the biggest, the grandest, the all we can know-the evolution of the universe.

The universe is a composite of all the bits of matter and energy that are now in existence. Religions defined the birth, the beginning, the creation, as the Genesis, which is the creation of everything with a definitive start initiated by the hands of a creator. For religions the time of Genesis is not well defined on any time scale and most dating attempts from a religious point of view have only led to more questions.

The Origin point for sciences is a supposed site of creation and time zero on a universal clock, which is defined as the big bang. Those bits of matter and energy both the light and the dark kind came into being following an evolutionary period immediately after the instance called the big bang. Now that start, the big bang, is a scientific conjecture, maybe a good one, but a conjecture nonetheless. The current scientific studies of cosmology and astronomy show that the universe is expanding. These studies are on very firm ground with extensive observations and data collection to back them up. Assuming that the current rate of expansion is constant, one can then calculate backwards and deduce that there was a time when everything in the universe was at one small point. That start time is calculated to be 14.2 billion years ago. Actually little if anything is known about this super condensed start-point and absolutely nothing is known about what preceded it. And what's more calling that initial event a big bang was a very poor name for a very serious origination theory for the universe. Just goes to prove that scientists and philosophers are as flippant as any other common guy when it comes to naming something they know so little about.

Regardless of the name, the big bang theory provides a good explanation for the start and the continued developments of our current physical universe. It provides a good explanation for how all the things we observe today may have come into being. This theory proposes that it wasn't long after that creational start that matter coalesced with the force of gravity and the universe became a birthplace for galaxies and stars. Within those early stars only hydrogen, a bit of helium and pure energy were the building blocks of matter. Eventually the stars created the elements, first a lot more of the elemental helium and then the heavier elements up to the element, iron. It was only when the really big giants of stars exploded in super novae that the heavier than iron elements like uranium were formed. This study of the physical world is known as physics.

Scientists have conclusive evidence and very good mathematical explanations for the method of formation for all the elements in the known universe. But the details surrounding the big bang starting point is still conjecture. What was around and outside of that starting point? What started that infinitely small point to expand? What, who, if anything, started the expansion? How could all matter, all energy, all stars, all galaxies in existence now be in one small point back then? It sure is something that is difficult for one to get a mind around. At first there was a void with one infinitely small point of everything yet to be. Then it became something-the universe with all its swirling stuff. Something was created and evolved to fill a void - wonder how that happened? Beats the hell out of me! Enter the supernatural and religion.

How could that infinitely small point contain all the atoms, electrons, protons, and all that other stuff that we now learn about in chemistry and physics? Do we see anything else, have any evidence, any scientific laws, anything, anywhere that something, somewhere, has been created out of nothing? A scientist would be the first one to say that can't be done. There are some things we don't know, may never know, and in fact some of which we are physically incapable of ever knowing. So let's set those questions aside for now into that arena that we call the metaphysical, the supernatural, the realm of religion and deal only with what we know. We cannot ignore the supernatural but we can set it aside for the present. Choose to deal with it later.

The universe is a single, speed of light expanse that is necessary for human existence. The universe created our Sun, the planets and the blue sea Earth particularly for us - or so we think. The universe neither commands nor judges our existence but mandates that we live in all respects to its natural laws. The search and understanding of natural laws increases our chances for survival and continued existence. To date and for all intents and purposes, humans are unique. We seem to be the most magnificent of all creation. So when we make a judgment on the evolution of the universe we have to say it has been good. Good for me, good for you, good for all mankind.

That evolution of the universe has been proceeding for 14.2 billion years and after a cracker-jack start has become slow and steady. Atoms were created within the first hour after the big bang. Stars, galaxies and planets not long thereafter but why pray tell did it take every bit of 14.2 billion years to make man? With its present movements the universe is expected to continue unabated for another trillion of years or more. So even if in the big scheme of things humankind was a long time coming it is indeed a biological and evolutionary miracle with lots of time ahead. We have been created to live in this universe and that for us is a good thing. Even if we factor in the universe's indifference to human concerns and objections about evolution.

Perhaps some simple explanations of commonly used but not really understood terms are needed. Let's start with nature. Nature needs to be understood as something infinite in space and time as well as in content and substance. Nature is something that is everything, everywhere, at the current time. Man is totally dependent on nature for his life, his existence, his very essence. Man cannot separate himself from nature and all of nature that makes up his substance. Ultimately every human life is the relationship between one's self and nature. Nature is everything man knows or can know. Nature in the broadest sense is the natural, physical and the material world or even more definitively, it is the universe at the present time. Today the simple fact remains we do not know all we need to know about nature. Nature becomes a present-day explanation of the workings of the universe. The universe is evolving so nature becomes the present-day totality of that which has evolved from the beginning.

For what it's worth let's consider an all-in cracker-barrel explanation of the connection between the universe, Genesis, big bang, nature, evolution and self. Five straight forward declarative sentences cover it all. Namely:

- The universe is everything there is, was, or ever will be.
- The Genesisor the big bang was the start depending on your view.
- Evolution is the process by which the universe changes millennium by millennium, year by year, second by second.
- Nature is the present state of that evolutionary process.
- The self's ultimate consciousness and awareness is the relation of a human being to nature.

So let's leave that which did happen as a creational start and what is continuing to happen to be something we refer to as evolution. We need to keep an open mind and be objective as we try to make sense of things.

≈

EVOLUTION OF THE SOLAR SYSTEM, THE SUN AND DIRT

The universe is believed to be 14.2 billion years old. The solar system with the Sun and the planets is not quite five billion, merely one third the age of the universe. For whatever the reason it took almost ten billion years of space-time to elapse and evolve before this section of interstellar space particular for us to begin a collapse. Under the force of gravity the mass it contained coalesced in a spiral disk fashion to ignite a solar nuclear furnace we now call Sun. The left-over bits of spiraling matter that didn't fall into the Sun accredited along a single saucer-like plane to unite into the large solid or semisolid bodies we call planets. It formed the four rocky ones closest to the Sun we named Mercury, Venus, Earth, and Mars. Also formed further away were four larger cold gas giants we named Jupiter, Saturn, Neptune, and Uranus. Each planetary mass cooled, create moons and took on a specific unique evolutionary nature of its own.

The solar system has those eight planets and many, many moons and even more comets and asteroids. All made of the same building block materials and all accredited at the same time and now have evolved and existed through the same duration of time. But the final products are vastly different depending upon a distribution of materials and individual methods of evolution. Even if we consider only our own solar system, Earth is still very unique to have evolved with a watery surface. The physical events that led to the formation and evolution of Earth are to itself phenomenal. Only Earth has an abundance of oxygen and liquid water evolved to permit advanced forms of life to exist.

We know Earth evolved to attain its present size and solar location about 4.5 billion years ago. Earth became a planet it is today through an extraordinary and elaborate sequence of evolutionary events. Its fiery and harsh beginnings left it sterile when first formed and for a long cooling period thereafter. It also went through numerous periods of starts and stops of primitive life emergence. For its own reasons and with time enough, the Earth has successfully become the home to an abundance and wide variety of life. Only Earth has advanced intelligent life. In the bigger scheme of things there can be little doubt that Earth is a charmed planet.

Earth is a remarkable mixture of land and water in a balancing act with a nitrogen and oxygen enriched atmosphere. Land formation on Earth has been created by two principle means-volcanism and plate tectonics. The continents formed when relatively low-density materials, the silicates, could permanently "float" on the denser underlying iron-rich mantle like a slag on molten iron. When things cooled the Earth's waters filled the basins around those rising continents of slag.

The Earth's earliest life in its most primitive makeup seems to have formed soon after the cessation of heavy asteroid and meteorite bombardment. Heavy cosmic barrage ended about 3.8 billion years ago followed by a rapid cooling process. Surprisingly we find evidence of the first semi-fossilized life imprints from some 3.5 billion years ago. Evidence points to microbial life beginning its existence as soon as Earth's environment made it possible. Scientist believe as soon as 700,000 years after solidification.

The evolution of larger and more complex life occurred much, much later in Earth's evolutionary history.

Noteworthy those earliest of fossils bear a striking similarity to bacteria still on Earth today. Yet there remains a lot of controversy on fossil remains and the significance to man. Let's set that controversy aside. Too much of that discussion lies in the realm of conjecture and as such will not be made a confrontational part of this story.

Life in fact was created here on planet Earth. The most important-first step was the creation of DNA, life's most basic information center. Followed in time was the origination of a sex-related domain (Eukaryote). The creation of two sexes further stoked the many fires of diversification. Specifically from these two phenomena the two great Kingdoms of flora and fauna were formed and flourished. The other three great Kingdoms of Monera (bacteria), Protista (algae) and Fungi showed little innovative or advanced evolution and lag behind, remaining the simplest forms of life even today.

Yet another of Earth's evolutionary charm that was needed for advanced life forms to exist was an atmosphere with sufficient oxygen. It took another 3.9 billion years and almost 85 percent of Earth's 4.5 billion years of age for there to evolve a suitable level of oxygen in the atmosphere. We now marvel at that age as the Cambrian to which many, many fossils give evidence. The Cambrian diversification of life forms came about due to that very important evolutionary attainment of oxidative metabolism. Oxidative metabolism in lay man's terms means how a body creates its own energy to exist and thrive. Even today it is important that Earth's atmosphere be continually replenished with that essential oxygen. Without an oxygen-enriched atmosphere larger animal never could have evolved. The metabolism of warm-blood animals requires a constant supply of oxygen. It is their energy source. It is why all advanced forms of life need oxygen to breathe to live. Even fish extract oxygen from sea water through their gills for energy production. For humans any more than eight minutes without oxygen and all life systems shut down.

But let's take a giant step back to the formation of our planetand consider only the surface of our planet and its most important constituents - dirt and water. Let's consider dirt first. Earth has been orbiting the Sun whose energy output has been relatively constant for billions of years. Benign conditions of the solar system and the Sun have continued for a long period of time that made advanced life possible. Humans as the most intelligent, advanced and precocious life form insists on cool clean water to drink. We champion pure air to breathe. But we take for granted dirt.

When mankind looks for real permanence, he will carve it in the very hardest of dirt that is stone. From the earliest of time whether it be a spear-point, an ax, or cave etchings and figurines, natural stone was the material of choice. Even today modern man will use Earth's basic materials for durability of products or for art when permanence is sought. Even cement and concrete are man-made stone. Marble, bronze, iron, steel and gold are materials of choice that are extracted naturally from the Earth.

Man delights himself with combinations of materials for endurance. In artistic endeavors man's material of choice has resulted in some fine statues mostly of himself, of course. There is the Venus DE Milo, the David and the Thinker. A beautiful female, a male Adonis and a bare-ass guy deep in thought. We spend our life searching for beauty, pleasure and knowledge always thinking of perfection.

Probably the best illustration of man's co-existence with nature is Auguste Rodin's bronze statue of the Thinker. The Thinker is a male nude sitting on a cold, hard stone with his chin resting on one hand and deep in thought. The Thinker according to Rodin was a representation of the Italian poet Dante Alighieri.

Supposedly the Thinker's thoughts were of the episodes that Dante experienced in the Divine Comedy. Dante's search of chaos to order, despair to hope, darkness to light and the prison of self to liberty of individuality. A man's transition from the Inferno to Purgatory to Paradise.

But are we not all thinkers? At least we should be. Some more than others - yet some not at all. Those who care not to think, act accordingly and heedlessly.

Today we view the Thinker as representing philosophy and knowledge. But is it not interesting that the Thinker is sitting on his bare behind and not standing? He is not looking to the Heavens but has firmly placed his butt on a rock of earthen bronze. Is it being nude that makes him think? Is it sitting on a stone-cold hard mass that makes him a thinker? Is it being a human with a brain that makes him a thinker? Or might it be as mundane as being stripped nude and wondering who was the low life that stole his clothes?

What about the artist's choice of a rock as structure for the Thinker. Not many consider the rock that the Thinker is sitting on to be of significance but maybe we should. We pay so little homage, reverence, tribute, honor and adoration to our Earthen sphere. And unfortunately, if you do worship our sole life-giving sphere of dirt, water and air it's considered pagan and heathen-go figure?

We owe the Earth a lot more respect. There is nothing more enduring or stronger or more stable than stone. Our Earth is a rocky planet with its stone and dirt enduring eons of stability. One that supports our feet and produces the sustenance to feed and maintain our very life. A stone may have no life-a stone has no thoughts, yet a stone exists and was created. Out of space and from dust did all adhere. Earth was a solidification of matter well before humans mattered.

Before I leave Dante's Thinker on his behind, let me say that we must recognize that our own thoughts are ephemeral and fleeting. Human life is so short on time. The stone, the Earth, we stand on is solid and enduring. Yet so often we regard the Earth as dirty, filthy, sooty and loaded with germs, deadly bacteria and sickness. It is either messy black gumbo or a muddy foul slop sticking to the bottom of our shoes. Take Earth's carbon, it always is sort of a hodge-podge union, especially in the human structure and composition. The human body is a messy conglomerate of complex carbon compounds and not the one that the carbon atom can make itself into with perfection of structure to become a perfect diamond whose hardness and clarity we cherish-pure carbon, nothing but highly ordered pure carbon. Our carbon is all tied up in almost undecipherable, complex, raunchy compounds. We are dirt mixed up with minerals, amino acids, proteins, DNA, RNA, neurons and synapses. Most of us have little clue on how we got made or need to know how we work and how we function. We are plagued by other carbon compounds that cause disease, measles, Ebola and cancers. We counter the bad carbon attacks by concocting drugs and pills and prescriptions of yet other forms of organic complexity mimicking or counter-acting evolution finest efforts. Carbon dioxide is especially besmirched as the main culprit of global warming. So few stop to think that with every breathe that we exhale, carbon dioxide is what the human body exhales out to the Earth's atmosphere as garbage. It is more than autos, busses and trucks whose exhaust is foul.

The Earth is constantly evolving creating new dirt with each lava flow. Changing continental formations with each move of plate tectonics. Creating beautiful gems or petrifying a tree or fossilizing a dinosaur with pressure and time. I'll end this devotion to planet Earth with a nod to climate change with a view from the big scheme of things. Climate change is Mother Nature's way-fire or ice-fry or freeze. We need but common-sense observation to acknowledge that many factors enter into climate and weather but all are evolutionary processes. All are needed to understand Earth's changing atmosphere. The Earth has a climate that waves back and forth from steamy tropical heat to icy freeze. A Earth's history of climate and plate tectonics that can deposit sea shells high upon hill tops and make dry land into seas and swamps.

Earth is not an absolute. It is not always a steady Eddie. It wobbles and weaves. It has precession around its axis. It has cycles as simple as heat of day and cool of night. Yet it is not Earth's cycles that are in real control.

The significant player in the greater scheme of climate change is the Sun. We need to acknowledge; we need to acquiesce to its power in all things large and small. Our life and death depend upon whether nine minutes ago the Sun's furnace shut down.

Each and every day, fifty percent of Earth is bathe in sunshine, fifty percent in dark. This has been going on for some four and a half billion years and counting. This Sun to Earth relationship has been a daily variation of climate change from heat of day to cool of night. The Sun can and does create havoc with temperature changes of ten to fifty or more degrees each and every day. Most of which is far from truly accurate predictions from one day to the next and definitely not controllable.

The Sun also has its own evolutionary variables. Variables so great to make man's efforts or contributions insignificant to climate change. The blip of a sunspot or a cosmic ray burst can show whose boss. The Sun we know can expand and contract - albeit slowly, very, very slowly. Slowly but eventually its nuclear furnace will be overridden by the even greater force of gravity. Gravity will ultimately rule in this evolutionary process. That thankfully and fortunately for us is a long time off. But in the meantime the Sun will continue to control. It will continue to cause ice ages, extinctions and die-offs or to continue with mainly benign conditions. Things could happen that are not caused by man nor of human blame. It is the constancy or the variation in solar radiation that plays the most important, all controlling natural climate consistency or variability on planet Earth. It is its evolution of changing hydrogen to helium eventually to the formation of iron that will expend all of Sun's energy and lead it to its cold dark evolutionary ending.

Now should man be prudent and watchful? Yes of course! Let us be intelligent and wise. Let us not be dogmatic and blindly righteous. Let us continue to take a proper and realistic direction with conservation and preservation. Climate change is certainly a scientific fact. Evidence suggests that its magnitude is modest, its progress is slow and adapting to the change can be made sensibly.

The extent to which humans are responsible for climate change is outweighed by climate system's own variability. Above all let us not let foolish foreboding run or ruin our lives. When it comes to competing with the Sun, man may tweak a bit here and there, but tweaking is about all he can really do. Unhelpful alarmism prevents us from focusing on smart solutions for human improvement. We need to avoid expensive, feel-good measures that have imperceptible climate adjustment. The Sun is in the full command and control mode and Earth we hope to stay steady. A sensible precept "be careful" should dictate policy. We need to understand that Mother Nature is not nice. Sun and Earth dance in space, sometimes a waltz, sometimes a rumba. If we but think clearly enough, we find the universe cares little for human tweaking.

The warming rate of world's average temperature, as we have all noticed, has slowed down to virtually nothing in the past fifteen to twenty years. Global warming has taken a hiatus if not a slight reversal. Yet it still is wise to pay attention and continue to cut emissions. But to curtail the full use of fossil fuels is to hurt the poor and those struggling to reach a modern standard of living. Fossil fuels are the cheapest and most efficient forms of pure energy - pure fact. It was fossil fuels and fossil fuels alone, that drove the energy engine of America's prosperity. Solar, wind, alternate energy sources are technologically expensive. Put ideals aside, we should continue to seek cleaner coal and fossil fuel usage. We should at the same time encourage the switch from coal to gas in the generation of electricity. We should encourage nuclear and develop cheaper solar and expand the technology of electrical storage. Wisdom for mankind is held by his technology and not in those monomaniacal movements that insist on immediate moves to only renewable energy schemes. Mankind's standard of living is linked to cheap energy, especially and principally the poorer folk. Mankind is dependent upon energy-technology is his way to match his living needs to nature's provisions.

Let's put this topic into a sensible perspective. Earth's climate is an enormously complex system which until the recent decade or two the term "as unpredictable as the weather" was used to deny the ability to predict most anything. Climate science is still in its infancy. As with the essence of all scientific inquiry there is always more to learn. Science takes time. Climatology is only about 170 years old. With so many questions still unanswered, why are so many politicians, the main-stream media and poorly informed individuals involved in demonstrations and taking hard-core stance for or against global-warming?

≈

Don Erdek

BILLUMS CREEK

I four-wheel it down the hill and across the lower forty acres of Dande ranch. Down to the edge of Billums Creek where Earth's water is so natural and clear. Billums is just a gentle Texas creek flowing due north in an uncharacteristic manner to join the Neches, a large peaceful river that has a southern flow as it heads to the Gulf of Mexico. Billums is always a pleasure, never a disappointment, when watching its steady flow and its waters cascading over mild drop-offs.

Shoes off, pants off, I slip down the embankment to the water's edge. Immerse myself in its waters to discover a hermitage, a Shangri-La, an escape to seclusion. Then I kneel in the waters of Billums and to its homage I pray. It gently continues its flow past me on its way to those oceans of Earth. It cascades over sand grains, past clay banks on around any barrier rock. Eroding out banks and gouging out the white sandy bottom. Changing its course and finding the simplest of route. No imagination, no computation in deciding its elevation of flow, always dipping and descending. It must follow all of nature's laws and gravity's attraction. It follows nature's requirements so its molecules of water must be of the state as set by temperature. Earth's climate must be temperate for it to be liquid. Too cold it will be ice, too hot and it will be vapor.

Its speed of flow follows the laws identified by Sir Isaac Newton with mathematical precision of vectors and velocity. Its lifting and moving capacity depending on the inertia of energy and matter. Its force and its mass a mastery of nature but honorably yields its will to that of the nature's evolutionary direction. Depositing today many forms of debris. Only tomorrow to lift again in a move to the sea. It acknowledges not my presence, nor my existence. It cares not that I think nor that I know it is water and not vapor. It cares not that I live and breathe.

There is little doubt that Billums Creek's waters are as real as most everything on Earth. To me they transmit a wisdom of ages in the evolutionary process. From the stars and comets water was sent to Earth. Away from the fusion of the star called Sun it condensed and adhere to planet Earth. Its destiny, its evolution is here today in Billums Creek.

With my knees on the bottom of Billums I splash its waters on my face. Then bend over to drench and baptize my head and let its waters penetrate my brain. I like the feel, the coolness, the shower. It not only penetrates my skin but permeates deeply and tingles my mind. I can feel its power for its mystery to unwind. Certainly, intelligent me knows these molecules of water are but lifeless inorganic matter. Two hydrogen atoms and one oxygen tied by nature at an angle of 106 degrees with a mysterious hydrogen bond to link water molecule to water molecule and make it a liquid and not a gas in this earthly environ. Water is oxygen and hydrogen when together with carbon and nitrogen and some others makes up the greater part of me. So I wonder can it be that my own hydrogen, my oxygen, was once part of the sea. And my carbon was it once a blade of grass or a dead tree? And nitrogen was it for ages the greater part of Earth's air? And did they each separately once long ago wander up in Earth's atmosphere lose and free? Or to be Earth's dirt bound for ages and ages before reforming and evolving to become the human me? Is there then some god-like bond between these Billums Creek waters and me? Is there some knowledge I can gain from these waters? So I ask the elements, no one in particular, do these waters have a time-honored message for me?

An impulse urges me to just ease back. Letting my body lie down, flat on my back and become totally immersed in Billums waters. I feel a oneness with nature. I can feel Billums water caress my thighs, roll over my naked skin, massage liquid essence into relaxing pores. Penetrating deeply into my brain and on to my mind which senses it all. My being opens up to a communion. A meeting of the elements, a joining of nature's forces, a magical connection harking back to the sacred blessing of creation's launch. Swiftly my soul, my conscience, my inner sanctum, springs open to a link between me and these waters.

I certainly know that Billums Creek waters has a common bond to all of Earth, to the Sun, to the workings of the universe and to its very origin of the universe. I feel it wishes to share and extend this knowledge to me. I let my inner sanctum swing open and wait for an essence to surface.

"Who am I now'?

I am the waters of Billums Creek.

I am the water flowing between earthen banks of sand and clay.

Destined never in one place to stay.

My droplets of water most often crystal and clear.

Past your ranch, I flow down to the Neches and then on to the Gulf.

I pluck sediments and sands from earth's mass.

I dissolve its salts and separate the elements.

I'll nourish the sycamore whose leaves are so broad.

I'll water the cypress whose knees poke out bare and bald.

The deer, the raccoon, the panther, will stop to slake a thirst or to cool a body.

I'll scatter things along the way-anything in my path I'll push and roll.

My movement is sometimes devastation-sometimes in tranquil repose.

In finality into the seas I'll deposit my salts along with the matter that did not oppose.

I'll then escape ocean's grasp to the sky I'll boil only once again to then condense.

Maybe back to Billums Creek in my ancient recycle or into you to quench a thirst.

So by leaving all my salts and deposits back in the ocean with evolutionary time they will evolve to get saltier and saltier.

In many respects I am everlasting.

From comet to ocean to atmosphere.

Then hack again to droplets and gravity snare.

My round trips span the ages.

Each journey a new vista and a reach for different exotic places.

Of nature and its forces, just like you, I must abide.

It is nature who controls my destiny and is my guide.

Each day a new transition bound tight with the strings of tradition.

In my water you can see so much evidence for the age of the Earth and the story of evolution.

Today, yesterday, and the yet-to-be can all be seen or foreseen.

In my waters you can feel the forces of nature at work doing its finest to the same workings of the universe itself.

The wonderful force of gravity causes my flow creating my energy to move objects large and small.

Thermodynamic realities of my water to be liquid at Earth's temperature in temperate zones - frozen at the poles.

Earths near eternal layers of soil to be eroded by me over long, long periods of time.

Exposing today petrified wood from trees buried deep within Earth's evolving and ever changing the many layers of dirt.

That burial of trees happened millions of years ago before my flow in Billums began.

Trees that lived back then were forced by the evolving forces of nature to be submerged deep within the Earth.

What was that natural horrific event?

An event to cause the downing of a forest of healthy tree and bury them so quickly and under sediment so deep to block oxygen of the air or microbes of the soil to destroy the wood.

Wood that remained entombed for millions of years and time enough for nature to transpose the wood to stone.

Millions of years of burial time to slowly evolve and fossilize atom by atom the organic cellulose of wood to become stone in a perfection of form and structure and exact duplication.

Then centuries more to allow my creek waters to expose.

Such magnificent feats to be accomplished as natural fact of but given time enough to work the wonders of nature.

Reversal of organic wood to inorganic stone is one of the simplest of nature's evolving processes which on a much more complex level creates life itself with a process using a double helix of amino acids to one by one duplication on strands of DNA.

A process which takes one amino acid at a time from a chosen select of four to create the genes of lift itself.

How all these processes work one can only admire and increase the search to know.

For certain nature knows how to do it.

Even here in my water of Billums Creek you may find clear signs of human evolution and the closeness to nature that is both clear and true to your heritage.

Those many arrowheads and spear points that can be found tell a human story of evolution.

Native Americans crossed my waters hundreds and hundreds of years ago.

They roved, hunted and gathered at a level not much above humanity's most primitive beginnings.

The fossilized wood they found in my creek bed and in the surrounds they fashioned into objects for hunting and marauding.

Doing whatever it took to stay alive.

They knew not the age and the essence entombed in a fossilized piece of petrified palm but they knew it could be made into a fine killing dart.

Now in but a few hundred years there has been time enough and evolution enough for some assemblage of a civilization in which humans find themselves embedded.

To be frank humans have so for yet to go- yet to evolve.

The workings of nature will allow humans to evolve if they be observant and curious.

I am not alive but I function to all the same rules that all life must abide.

Adhere to those laws of nature that were created at the origin of all things.

To ignore the laws of nature and the ages before is to ignore the freshness and wetness of my waters.

One ignores the majesty of nature if time is not taken to think and ponder what is real and separate it from that which is not.

One must continue that search for what has been real since the beginning of time with all that has evolved since the origin of the universe.

But today there is a difference to my flow past this ranch called DANDE.

What is this entity, this obstacle, into my water did kneel?

Around it I must flow-is it a rock? A petrified bone? A new type of tree?

I do believe it may be the strangest of creature.

That evolutionary complex creation - yes, it is, a human he.

Is he John the Baptist in search of the Lord?

Is he searching for a spear point left by that moccasin man of the past?

Is he in search of the philosopher stone?

Or does he search for that shiny element of gold?

Does he even know of what he seeks?

If I were to guess it would be his penchant, his quest, for some beauty unknown.

Whatever his curiosity he will know my course is true.

My water he will find clear.

Whatever he searches for he just might find here.

Well now that was powerful. I need to get my aged frame out of this creek, I have wrinkles enough, I need no more. A lot for me to think about and ponder this natural interlude has surprises even for me. It shows that even a common guy can become a modern-day prophet when he goes in search for truths. Akin to a John the Baptist sitting in Billums baptizing one's self with worldly truths and a bit of the mystical. I now know I can meditate, I can medicate, I can smoke weed on the banks of Billums creek at sunset, or I can just be myself and let myself think. It becomes a splendid achievement to make a human smarter, one mind at a time.

≈

A FLORAL EXHALE FOR FAUNA LIFE

There is a copse of trees along both sides of Billums Creek are so dense that their tops join to shade the creek waters below. Nature has tossed a soft green cloak over this solemn place. This copse is a sanctuary, an edifice, a cathedral that nature built. A nature's place for refuge and solace. If there is such a thing as a haunted spot - this one is haunted. The eerie silence is so profound that as one stains to hear, it is only one's own blood pumping that one feels upon his inner ear. All the while the sun's rays pierce through the trees playing havoc with the other senses. The heavy floral growth creates a sanctuary of beauty and tranquility. The close-by waters of Billums Creek can be soothing and cool but these trees are spooky.

It is a spot like this that provokes mystery and allows one to gain a oneness with nature. So dissimilar to those deserts of choice by the long age prophets, but surely a place of repose for an intellect to think. Perhaps spirits of the Caddo Indians of centuries past move silently along these banks. The dim sun light strains and dances through the thick growth of leaves making phantom shadows like a slow soft step of moccasin clad feet. Today it is a solitary modern man who invades this sanctuary of photosynthetic evolutionary transformation.

As I ease into a reverie of silent introspection, I think is it not the Origin and evolution of all things that gave life to a tree? Certainly to me trees are a wonder. They give shade and verdant beauty for us humans to behold. Isn't it so nice that this good Earth was formed to hold green trees? These green trees stand with a firm root in the ground so unlike me who can move around. I so love the color green, probably because the green wave sets in the spectrum's center. Merely a wavelength of light that upon the human iris is seen as green, with the blue wave a bit shorter and the red wave a little longer. I wonder if mankind should declare the color green and not the color of skin as a true search for color equality.

A murmur, a whisper glided past my ear. A distinct voice I heard or was it but my soul seeking oneness with the copse of trees. I surely think I heard some thoughts coming not from within but from about.

You foolishly and naively came to this copse to be alone. But you are not alone. Each tree senses your presence here, monitors your actions, even captures your fleeting thoughts. We know things you are unaware of. We produce the elixir for your very existence. We are here for you or more pointedly you exist because of us. You are definitely barking up the wrong tree if you think it's the green color of trees that is important to you. It might really be a jolt to your own self-proclaimed human superiority if you but acknowledge the real importance of a tree For you see they were needed to create oxygen for you to breathe.

Now wait a minute! What does this have to do with trees? Wasn't oxygen preordained? Wasn't Earth's atmosphere created and baptized with oxygen by design? Wasn't that in the original design - wasn't it part of our destiny? Didn't oxygen come along with all of that other star dust and comet stuff that created my Earth? All a part of the Creator's plan.

Well yes and no! Way back when, at its start the Earth was much like any other planet with no suitable atmosphere for humans to breathe. And of course there were no trees. All carbon, all oxygen was all locked up in other solid rocks and things, none was left over to fill the atmosphere or create a tree. As a matter of fact it was like that for most of the 4.2 billion years of Earth's history. At the beginning there was no oxygen at all in the atmosphere and it required an evolutionary process for it to be created as part of earth's air. It took a long, long time and it was a slow, slow evolutionary process and trees and flora had to come first in the evolutionary plan.

That doesn't sound right! Why was it done that way? What was the reason that it took so long and why were trees needed? And why weren't we needed in the big scheme of things until so late in the game?

Maybe, just maybe, it was to humble you that the creator had as slower evolutionary plan and chose to give flora a place on Earth before it allowed humans to come into being?

Boy does that ever pinch my bubble! I like trees but that shoots the crap out of my ego. But before I start to worship bushes I think I'm going to go over to that tree right here and ask it a question or two. Hey tree, what kind of a tree are you and just where do you think you stand in the big scheme of things"?

Well I'm a Dogwood. I don't have a mouth to talk or a brain to think but I've been known to rustle a few leaves now and then. So if you listen closely as the good Earth s winds stir me I may shake and flutter and with rhythmic whispers, my story just might unfold. If you smell my blossoms when they bloom, they can touch a primordial sense within you and stir perceptions you may not know you have. Or right now touch my out-stretched branches for there-in reclines a rippling and resonate saga of the wisdom and majesty of one of nature's finest evolutionary creations. Set your eyes upon my leaves and see their composite, compound veins which carry nutrients, photosynthesis and life. I may not be able to move, but to you, you and all of mankind, I give my greatest of gifts. If you but come close and breathe deeply you will savor the flavor of my freshly created oxygen-just for you-all for you. I am here as part of a grand design-I am one of the nature's greatest evolutionary creation. That which created the universe and then evolved the Solar System, the Earth, and trees.

So yes, as you may know, I am of the kingdom of plants while you of the kingdom of animals. My genesis pioneered from an eukaryote cell that originated in the sea and then eventually conquered the fixation of chlorophyll. With chemistry, photosynthesis, evolution and the majestic rays from Lord Sun I begot my type of life. Later, much later, my genesis pioneered flora life on Terra Firma. My heredity on land and dirt dates to one billion years before the present. Your eugenics took some five hundred thousand years more to do the same. I do believe it was the need for my kind to fill the atmosphere with the oxygen essential for your kind to exist.

Yes, I am a simple Dogwood tree. And yes, I am living. I am alive and dance with the seasons of Mother Earth as we spin around Father Sun. My favorite, of course, is the springtime of blossom bloom. My DNA is made of the same components as yours. DNA in you, in me, in all living things made from a chosen four amino organics. Four nucleotides bases - adenine, thymine, guanine and cytosine. The order they take in helix form create a strand of DNA - the language of life · within the strands are the genes that code for all information about a particular life form. Many more bases there exist in the genetic code much of which is called junk - but personally I think not! Don't ask why? Don't ask how? Some things have a significance and are just meant to be. But our chromosomes and genes differ in number, differ in kind. A crazy thing this all may be, but it is so nonetheless. The Origin and its evolutionary methods chose what was best suited. Molded from what was here on Earth to bring to existence what needed to be. We need only to accept that you are you and I am me. Now what you need to know is that it is my photosynthesis that is so important and essential for you to live and breathe.

How important is photosynthesis? Very! The process is so successful that it is the foundation for nearly all/life on Earth. The rich ecosystem of plants and animals on Earth's surface all depend on sunlight. Sun's energy gets funneled to create chlorophyll through a chemical reaction that splits the water molecule and releases oxygen. Photosynthesis is the process that I use to take carbon dioxide from the air, water from the ground and then grab a photon of light from the sun. With that process I make my food, my sugars, my carbohydrate, my cellulose. But what is important to you is that as I use carbon dioxide from the air and water from the ground I also create and then freely release pure oxygen back to the air. So my photosynthesis and that of all flora maintain atmospheric oxygen levels and supplies all the organic compounds and most of the energy necessary for lift on Earth. We are the food, the vegetables, the leafy and the green for mammals of Earth to eat. We are the ones that fill the air with oxygen for mammals to breathe.

My kind began this process some 2 billion years ago during the Proterozoic era long before any mammals were conceived. Some of my very ancient ancestors are known to you and used by you as the vast beds of coal and fossil masses that lie deep in the Earth. In recent times trees are used to kindle a fire or to fashion a cross, or ignition to stoke a pyre. There are even poems and gospels, obituaries that include trees. We are old, very, very old and with trees there are old stories, there are fables, there are tales. Some of wonder-some of delight.

But there is one biblical fable that pains me most. For you often speak about man's inhumanity to man. But never a word when you cut down a tree. And here my tree tale begins. Two millennium ago, in a place called Judea lived the finest of my species. At the time the Dogwood grew straight and strong. One of my brethren you singled out for deadly and sinful duty. You chopped and quartered and fashioned three crosses and anchored them back on a mount called Calgary. At the center of those three to a Dogwoods dishonor you crucified a specially gifted human being.

The Dogwood has ever since bore the burden of that deed to us. The Dogwood was given no chance for repentance, none for redemption. No longer do we grow tall and straight--we pine and weep, stay stunted and short lived today. Let me leaf you with this thanatology. Search the heavens, Catch a comet by the tail, Get up close and personal to a tree, The solace and immortality you seek just might be firmly rooted in the dirt right here besides me. With my finest and most fervent flower power I bid you a deep fresh oxygen breath.

What can I say, I'm speechless. Puts more understanding to praying for rain and hoping trees and crops will grow and produce more oxygen. Humbling to say the least! Nothing like a tree giving a man yet another slant on nature and evolution. Although the dogwood didn't stress it, it is obvious there's also a need for more sensible discussions about carbon dioxide. Of all the world's chemical compounds none has been bad-mouthed more than carbon dioxide. Demonizing by single-minded advocates that carbon dioxide is a dangerous pollutant and strict government control of energy fossil fuels must be made mandatory with a goal to completely eliminate their usage. Completely ignored is that actually mild increases of carbon dioxide will actually benefit agricultural productivity and support the ever-increasing human population.

≈

THE JELLY FISH

A stroll on the beach.

Another wonderful day of my life.

The sun...the sky...the beach...the sea.

A bit of heaven...a day in paradise...all for me.

How wonderful a gift of Earth, the Stars, and the Infinite Cosmos all made for me.

The sky is blue, well not really, but that is how I see it.

The water is wet, well not really, but that's how I feel it.

The sand is crunchy, well not really, but that's how the Earth made it.

Things are what they are, well not really, but that's how we humans named them.

We named them so we can write about them and then you and I can know them.

We're really smart, well not really, but that's how we think of things we think we own.

We are the cream of the crop... the top dog... the ace of creation.

We know nature and we control it, well not really, we just think we do.

That's it "we think"..."we are aware"...we know things.

We tell the UNIVERSE we know you exist because I do.

You can't fool us humans because we are smart and we have a brain.

And you made us to think that you ain't nothing if you don't have a brain.

The leisure stroll over the sand and shells of Barefoot Beach continues before a step into the water.

Well lookie, lookie now ... what do we have here?

A big old jelly fish is up close floating by.

So I wade out into the water to close the gap.

I see him but he can't see me.

What a simpleton he seems.

I wonder what this jelly fish feels like.

I'm gonna catch him and hope he don't sting.

With wide open palms to its sides I squeeze.

Well damn I sense it.

There are distinctive shivers.

It is quivering with an unmistakable shake.

A primordial fear I surely awoke.

Alert, alert, my protoplasm is disturbed.

Something is threatening my space.

Must protect my gonads,

Must save the future,

Must continue the species, save the race.

I have no brain.

No soul do I seek.

But my will to live is buried deep.

No evolution.

No extinction.

My simple life becomes the eternal solution.

I know not of stars, galaxies and such.

But a disturbance to my field is caused by whatever that foreign touch

I must oscillate and undulate away from here.

But alas I cannot move.

A grasp from without seals my doom.

What does it want of simple me?

I threaten no one.

I'll tell you everything if only you will let me be. MUST OSCILLATE AND UNDULATE AWAY

Well damn again...I do believe those quivers, shivers, and shakes sent a message.

So let me squeeze again right here.

Somewhere in time and space did I come together?

I was given the right, the desire, and the drive to live.

In the simplest of body without a brain, living protoplasm my God gave to me.

His only demand of me is that I strive to live.

My pledge to him myself to replace.

How simple life can I be?

But that common drive, the will to live is buried deep.

As is that other urging, the need to originate another me.

Whence came that urge to live, that desire to bloom?

Was it not that touch from God, the Sun, the Earth and the Moon?

That will to live I hold dear.

How simple a creature I might be?

But pause and think is that not like thee?

I'll do my best to stay alive.
If but your grasp I can unfold.

I have no brain.
I cannot think or see.
A mouth I have but not fit to talk.

I know the cold.
I know the hot.
I have sensor and receptors to do the job.

Ocean currents cause me to sway.
I move with ease and love to be free.
This great big sea may no longer be for you but it is home to me.

I ingest, digest, absorb and go on.
I may not have pecs, hams, gluts, or lats.
I lack a spinal, dendrites and lobes.
No boobs or knockers, no keister or tokus.
But protoplasm I have as an organized mass.
With proteins, nucleus, plastids, I'm in my own special class.

Primordial urges within me stir.

Eggs or sperm the creator directs.

Into the ocean I must project.

A move to spew the essence of me.

Across time, from then to now, and onward to eternity.

His gift to me a life.

My curtsy must be a sacred honor to live well.

My movements are not dressed in robes of mathematical rigor.

I react to the vagary of waves and wind.

An unsuitable temperature I try to avoid.

A strange vibration a must to resist.

The grasp of your palms a danger, a hazard, a threat, a risk.

So if you can be so kind of the same life you hold dear.

Please let me go and relieve my consternation.

Your life… my life…a common creation.

So you go and do your thing and I'll do mine.

Unhand me, you brute

It's back to the sea for you.

There is more than room enough for the two of us here.

You need the water; the land is for me.

You continue your float in your time and space.

I'll resume my stroll.

≈

THE TURTLE

Here I am taking a stroll and walking the dog. A turtle I see or maybe he sees me. Nope he's tuck within his shell not a soul he sees but I see him. It's then I hear him say ...or is it but a telecommunication, telepathy or perhaps a reincarnation.

Why am I a turtle?

I move so slowly.

My shell is heavy but i need it.

My needs are few, only a morsel or two.

I don't have many thoughts; no more than I need.

Often I hide I have much to fear; although i know not of what or why.

What to do is all outside me; that is but for the times that I not hide within.

No words do I say, no bible written for me.

Who put me in this worldly shell, I cannot say.

I have no claim to fame; the sky was white when once I came.

Lineage I know not of that shell of the beginning I had to shove.

What to do; where to go; if it's chance alone then but a sorry, slow, show.

But here i am, even if I know not where.

So why am I here and should I care.

Do I even need to know what I'm to do.

Am I supposed to follow a path of good or of bad?

And if so what is that?

Am I to be gracious of life?

And if so what is gratitude and what is life?

Every so often I have a maddening itch.

A salve or soothing my creator did not provide; so suffer I must with that tingling twitch.

So why I am here and what am I to do?

Of that I know not of; but a drive it is I know exists.

Those drives...that endeavor to persist do within me silently insist.

Where did it originate?

Why so strong this insistence and the endeavor to persist.

So is life good. I cannot say...it's all I got and so carry that ever so strong wish to stay.

And yet another drive lurks within, it comes and goes is it a need to swim?

What drives me I know I'll find; I often wonder is it that itch that drove me to distraction?

For deep within is the surety that itch will become a drive and somehow an uncontrollable passion.

It is destined to happen that life's search becomes a rapturous journey?

A touching of another of like kind; a beholding of the face of god.

The endeavor to persist becomes a new beginning.

Well my dear turtle, I can call you but a shell of an entity but an entity no less. Within your shell lies a striving to persevere in your own being in what is your own life. You are a living organism and as all others, from protozoa to humans, are constructed and instructed by nature to maintain coherence of its life and its functions against numerous threatening odds to live and to recreate. To each his own, to each a part in evolution and perpetuation.

≈

ACTION OF A LESSOR GOD

A moment in time and a fine day for me to be sitting on a bench. A moment to spend with another animal, a dog, who without a doubt is man's best friend. Maybe because we made that so and then again maybe, but not likely, it was the choice of the gray wolf. For you see all dogs have been bred from the gray wolf. Take your pick of a dog: Great Danes, Chihuahuas, Poodles, Pit Bulls. They have all been man - made from the gray wolf. Hard to believe that several millennium ago there were no dogs. There was the wolf, the coyote, the jackal and fox but there were no dogs. Dogs were domesticated from the wolf starting around fifteen thousand years ago. "Domesticated," now that's a neat word, for humankind penchant to fool with evolution and make things nature did not make. Today dogs come in more varied shapes and sizes than any other mammal on Earth. They are a simple product of specific selection of offspring. All dogs are a genetic manipulation of the gray wolf by humans. Whether it is the huge lumbering Great

Dane or the testy manikin Chihuahua, it is man's recreation of the wolf. It is much like Menndel's alleles and using Darwinian present-day selection and evolution with mankind's hand at the control. I guess we could give reasons why this is so and why we did it and maybe just because we could like the actions of a Lessor God. The most valid and startling reason is that although we vaguely understood evolution at first we learn quickly that it can indeed be manipulated. Now a dog may not be able to play Texas Hold-Em. but everything else about dogs was done with intent. Wolves can't take a hint but dogs have evolved the ability to read their owners. Dogs are very good at understanding human voices and gestures.

It is even more amazing that most of the many, many breeds we know today did not exist as near as two thousand years ago. In fact over the last two hundred years it's been a fast track for manipulating how a dog should look. There is a clear lesson here on why humans may not be all that wise when it comes to evolution. Some of those pure-bred dogs may be cute or elegant but most lack a canine aptitude. Just compare those dogs of pure breeding with the dogs of uncontrolled breeding - those mutts - they are the smartest dogs of the whole lot. Something like their masters - we are all mutts. Might the lesson be that nature, the ultimate culler, does it best with mutts. This brings to the forefront the subject of "human changelings," the human mutts whether we came out of Africa or from the Garden of Eden. It begs the question just how fast human mutts are genetically changing because we are continually changing and changing fast. Significant evolutionary changes are not only possible but actual. Major evolutionary adjustments and changes to humans have occurred over the last fifty thousand years. Those changes are so obvious because people all look so different. Today when populations are separated by great distances or geographical barriers changes occur rapidly. Individual traits can be generated and reproduced quickly over relatively short periods of Earth time. No Chinese can be mistaken for a Caucasian. No African bushman for a Nordic. No Australian aborigine for a Scotsman. All these distinctive differences in appearance have both a genetic and an evolutionary explanation. Of interest to genealogy today are the changes to the genome as man evolves from hunter gatherer to an agriculture, industrial, technological society. Radical changes to the genome must be occurring with the transition and its developing social institutions, especially religion and government. We are born with a genome but it is ever evolving and must he greatly affected by these new needs for the fusion and the continued existence of vast numbers of peoples living together in choice locations.

And then there is an even more startling genetic and evolutionary effect from about 50,000 years ago. At that time Neanderthal man shared this planet with our own Homo-Sapiens. In Europe for 5,400 years, and probably much longer, Homo-Sapiens and Neanderthal co-existed. No hanky-panky. Well, think again. Same equipment you know. Regardless that we may have a visceral reaction to this idea, genetic markings show that some of us especially Europeans carry about 4 percent Neanderthal genes. I guess there are some things better not to know or acknowledge.

Now here is a near-on unbelievable slant on an evolutionary connection between Neanderthal, Homo Sapiens, the gray wolf, and dogs. In a very recently published book by Pat Shipman titled "The Invaders" she discusses how Homo Sapiens and their wolfdogs helped drive Neanderthal to extinction. The bones of wolfdogs have been found at human burial sites but not at any Neanderthal sites. Ms. Shipment proposes that Homo Sapiens domesticated the wolfdog, but Neanderthal did not. She cites a very unique explanation for this that is quite startling. In any event that alliance of Homo Sapiens and the wolfdog gave Homo Sapiens a distinct advantage. The wolfdog became a fellow predator who was able to run faster, see and smell better, ward off enemies and guard encampments. Ms. Shipment contends that this synergistic pairing tilted the balance in favor of Homo Sapiens. That body feature specific to Homo Sapiens and not Neanderthal I leave for you to uncover in Ms. Shipman's book, so you may judge for yourself her contention.

So go pet a dog. They love us unconditionally with so much happiness, contentment, and joy. If only we humans could feel and show those emotions as quickly and as easily as a dog does. A simple wag of a dog's tail says it all. And it matters not to them how poorly we treat them or forget to feed them. Nor how badly we messed up their natural ancestry to that majestic creature, the gray wolf. If ever there was a forgiving animal it is the dog. No matter what your actions or for how long you ignore or neglect them they are always so happy to see you again with a tail wag that shakes their whole body. And their fascination with keeping eye contact with humans is phenomenal. Whereas with all other animals, human eye contact causes distress, anxiety, or immediate hostility. But dogs watch us all the time looking for approval or simply being curious to what we are doing. They will tilt a head to try and understand what we are saying. They know a happy voice from a scolding one. The most intelligent of them respond to hand signals alone, knowing with a simple hand gesture or with the quick read of body language what is expected of them. They are excellent people readers.

Time to get off the bench, fetch the dog and continue my role as a Lessor God.

≈

THE HUMAN ANATOMY

Living organisms had bodies long before they had brains. They had mechanisms to continue life and solve problems automatically with no proper reasoning required for survival. We humans share much the same basic survival mechanisms for our individual life. Let me once again present an all-in cracker barrel statement about the human body with but five simple declarative sentences of the body's needs. Namely:

- We need to find a source of energy-food.
- We must incorporate and transform that energy for power and locomotion.

- We must maintain a chemical balance of the interior life process.
- We must maintain the body's structure by repair of wear and tear.
- We must fend off external agents of disease and injury.

All you need to know about the human body you can find in Grey's Anatomy. All the controversy on evolution you can find in the Bible or in Charles Darwin's "Origin of Species." All I know is that you are born with what you got, so make the most of it. Let me state what I believe to be an absolute truism about the human anatomy. I am in my skin-only if I jump out can any other jump in.

None of us humans are equal, have never been equal, will never be equal. We are all different. We are all separate individuals. We exist in different bodies and occupy a different place in space and time. Each individual's DNA proclaims it to be the creation of a genome structure like no other. Finger prints say so with whorls and loops of individuality. Eye iris say so with a pattern of exclusivity. Our individual intelligence say so with thoughts shared with no one else. Our individual genes and nature make each of us different. Different parents, different dates of birth, different upbringings, different friends. The billions of humans living today are all different. Not one in the innumerable Homo Sapiens of yesteryear were the same. To make humans equal in some future world would be disastrous for the species. No one, not now, not ever are equal in anatomy. Male and female but the most obvious inequality in physical make-up and structure. That was one of nature's first great divide, two sexes, a split in half, a divide by two. What a marvelous construct. What an innovation. Sex is evolution's most magnificent, most enduring, most valuable discovery. Sex is the ability of organisms to specialize into a male and a female variety. Sexual reproductions first appeared about a billion years ago. At the most primitive and basic level cells show separation between male and female. It is common knowledge that cells contain chromosomes and it is on this level that separation into male and female occur. Clearly distinguished by females having two copies of the

X-chromosome, while males have one X and one Y

chromosome. The how or why can be debated but its importance and longevity to life's continuity and success is indisputable. Sex is one of nature's greatest evolutionary fast tracts to man's destiny.

The everything, the all, the essence of all we know, all that we know not of, is in this one anatomy. Nothing can be greater to us than to have been born. We humans on this precious Earth find our body so placed. We are but a speck in an infinite expanse of space. We are not on center stage in the big scheme of things. And we don't even know if there exists a center stage. Yet here we reside in this comfortable place we call Earth. Yes, our bodies belong here and nowhere else. We lack any assurance that any more than Earth was made for us. We can't even assure ourselves that nature or the greater universe even cares if we live or die. We like to think we matter but have so little proof.

Human life - my life - your life, we so often ask what part does humanity play in the big scheme of things? Each life is bound on either side by the endlessness of time before and the unfolding of ages ahead. Those billions of years of star dust before and to be Earth dirt again at some date in the future lays little claim to the pretense of importance of self. All the time before a nonexistence, not a clue we have of a previous time. All that time to come an enigma, a mystery, that will be without the body of me. That's what makes today, the time you are here, residing in a solid body, as solid as it ever will be. Life is what it is and not something you hoped it to be. The body is limited by so much. The speed of light, the eternity of time, the infinity of space, the unseen powers of matter and energy. The frailty of the body frightens me.

≈

Don Erdek

THE WILL TO LIVE

Let me unequivocally state that the human brain is a most rare and wondrous oddity in the universe. The human brain is one of the most complex objects in the universe. It contains a hundred billion neurons and has close to a quadrillion connections. The gray matter of the brain is highly malleable and responds to all sorts of signals from the world outside of it. If for no other reason this is a truly great reason to celebrate mankind's position in the universe. For you see mankind's existence does not reside "out there" or "up there" or in the mind of a Deity, but right here in this small mass we humans carry in our cranial cavity.

We humans share an obligation to be as intelligent as possible. We need to make sense of the world around us. We need to understand how we fit into the big scheme of things. We share this endeavor with all those living today, with those distant ancestors before, and all others who walk upright both in body and thought.

The primary function of the brain is to keep tabs on what goes on at all times in the rest of the body. The brain must also keep tabs about the environment surrounding the body So that suitable and serviceable accommodations can be achieved. The brain at all times must be vigilant and attend to the proper maintenance and functioning of the body in which the brain resides. The heart must beat, the self must eat. Always alert to the realization that if there is no body, there is no brain.

The body has a brain; the brain through consciousness develops a mind. The mind progressively develops awareness to further enhance the being's existence. A simple definition of consciousness is an individual's awareness of its self and the self's surroundings. Most mammals have consciousness and memory but humans have greater magnitude and higher degree of worldly wisdom. Consciousness in humans is multi-layered. Those layers are both simple and complex. The most basic and simplest consciousness is being aware of the present, the moment, the here and the now. Complex consciousness includes memory of the past and anticipation of the future. With a big brain, humans have developed the capacity for extensive record keeping of personal experiences. With human communicative abilities comes an ability to learn from others, so very important to acknowledge this is done one human, one brain, one mind at a time.

In a nutshell, consciousness is knowledge being obtained by the five senses and fed to the brain. Knowledge is the memory and organization from the body's sensors that form into an ever expanding and processing mind. The greater the knowledge accumulated the more adept the individual. Even the arts emanate from the mind's reading of the sensory input and merging them with the entities inborn genetic factors. This explanation of consciousness is an oversimplification. Consciousness does not fully explain the human mind in the big scheme of things. For there is that greater level of awareness that is attained through increased knowledge. Some individual are fortunate to be born with more intelligence, a higher capacity and thus greater ability to gain knowledge. In most instances the average individual must strive harder and dedicate more effort in their life to attain that higher level of awareness. It is with all extended awareness that allows a human brain to reach its very peak of mental and physical abilities. The ability to create things, helpful things, artistic things. The ability to consider the mind of another. The ability to sense the minds of the collective. The ability to experience joy, to suffer through grief. The ability to value life. The ability to sense and share beauty. The ability to know the inevitability of death to one's self and that of others. In all this what particularly deserves to be highlighted is the need for the body, the brain, the mind to be self-reliant and responsible to it. It takes years of careful and deliberate nurturing for anyone brain to reach peak efficiency.

Consciousness becomes an irresistible urge to stay alive. It is the key to an examined life and to the development of a concern for one's own life. To know about hunger and thirst, love and sex, tears and laughter. To develop a concern for others and to improve the quality of life. To have feelings and emotions and to seek a greater meaning to life. To have developed language and stories, science and philosophy, music and poetry, sadness and happiness, pain and ecstasy, glory and defeat. And then to continue to amplify all these for better or worse. But humanity's greatest accomplishment came with the evolution and development of a superior awareness. This superior awareness was many degrees higher than any previous conscious abilities, this

is mankind's amazing and enigmatic conscience. So synergistically along with that increase level of knowledge an individual develops the deepest, the purest, the truest conscience.

Most all individuals have awareness, not all develop conscience, and even fewer seek an even deeper meaning to life. Consciousness is not conscience. Consciousness does not explain the soul. In addition, there are good and bad states of consciousness. Most criminals are not consciously impaired; their conscience is an inner sanctum they definitely lack.

Yet there is more, much more, much greater. There resides in each of us the possibility to use our superior awareness and our conscience to search for a truly human connection to all of nature and to all the natural laws that govern the universe. To reach a pinnacle of truth that extends to each individual who seeks distinctiveness. If there is any quality universal to all humankind, it is the oneness with the universe. For a human it requires a brain and a developing mind. One must use these facilities to extend awareness that seeks a oneness with the universe. A human who develops his superior awareness and then reaches out beyond Earth and to understand natural laws and search for a connection may find something that pervades everything that exists. It is that oneness, that quality in a conscience that searches for deeper meaning that is perfectly captured by what I refer to as an inner sanctum. The inner sanctum is a precocious perception needed to find the goodness in man. Prophets searched for it in earthly deserts. Saints are easily guided through life on its goodness. Most of us have it to a more or lesser degree. A few, a very few, have none of it or lost it and have no desire to look for it. In effect I now raise my consideration of the level of importance I give to my own soul.

A mystery still lies ahead in the relationship between inner sanctum and society. That relationship lies somewhere beyond incompletely understood and difficult to explain. In any event it must be continually pushed on and beyond in an evolutionary quest to understand and develop the possibility that there exist a universal inner sanctum pervading all there is. So we must continue the search for knowledge using the many ways we know how. With the use of our brains, we today and many of those before, have noticed the rhythmic patterns in the sky and of the land. The display of order and regularity in nature is obvious to any that pay attention.

How can we not notice day from night, seasons and tides, a moon with phases, planets that revolve, life cycles of plants and animals, gestation periods, life and death and all the many wonders of nature. All these are trends and happenings in our world that move in their own particular way without human intervention.

For many of us it has become an obligation to search for the meaning of life. The universe may be huge but we know for certain that Earth is the planet especially adapted and ideally suited for humans or conversely we for it. It is with the human brain that each of us looks for an answer to our life, to why we exist and to acknowledge that we appreciate our existence. This universe, this Earth, this mind has to mean something really, really important with a purpose and a connection.

So we need to use our brain in a way that is true to self as well as with those things and others who are not us. We must acknowledge that even though others are not me, they and me are of a purpose. A purpose that depends on one another for mutually enhanced existence. For communal life among human a set of moral codes and a virtuous life is needed. It is to our own individual brains that one must be true to find the greater purpose.

We must define the obligation that each individual has to its own life. Overall the most important occupation of the human mind is the relationship of the human mind to nature. The mind exists because there is a body to sense-if there is no body, there is no brain, no mind. Might the mind be servant to the body rather than vice-versa? Long before living organisms had brains, they had devices and mechanisms to solve problems of survival automatically with no reasoning. They needed no thought to maintain survival of the individual life. Still today that survival mechanism flourishes-grab an earthworm and see it squirm. So it seems these basic survival mechanisms reside in the DNA genome before it became a complex reaction with a brain to regulate.

There is in each and every living organism the relentless endeavor to preserve itself A striving and natural tendency to seek both survival and well-being. There is that drive to preserve one's self come what may until life is suspended by aging, disease, or externally inflicted

injury. We all know how difficult it is to watch or see a loss of life. There is a haunting and deep-down disruption of our inner being at that moment of necessity to put an old dog down or end the life of a too sick cow.

It is so important that we pay attention to things that motivate like beauty, love, magic, mystery and grandeur. Then to add poetry, delicacy, refinement, purity, splendor, intimacy, innocence, fulfillment and inspiration. Moving on with the nuances of drama, integrity, and harmony. The world in which we dwell offers a shared spectacle of limitless images, constant banter, endless noise, infinite information and mountains of new facts. All of this can be a stimulus or a narcotic or sometimes a distraction to purpose. Each of us knows how vulnerable life can be and how necessary our mind is to our basic survival. Life may have been given to us;

survival is not. Our body is given, its sustenance is not. The body with the brain is used to sense, perceive, identify and integrate the world we are born into. Our brain is given to use, however its content need to be individually maintained, sustained and supplemented. Knowledge is necessary for survival. Reason and logic is the means to gain that knowledge.

Our knowledge increases from day one, hour one, minute one, second one, if not from that all before in the DNA and genome. To think with a purpose is to incorporate the world around us into the cells of our brain to create a mind. Reality becomes all that which enters the brain and is organized in one's mind. It is your life, your reason to live, your purpose to add meaning to nature for the gift of life. With age, knowledge should become precious wisdom.

To remain alive we must act and think. To act properly we must know nature. Man keeps his body alive through nutrients, his food. He knows what type of food is good and learns the proper way to obtain it. To continue to persist he must obtain knowledge by thinking. The grandest of human achievement is our scientific accomplishments. It is our collective ability to create knowledge through the human intellect. It is a joint effort to understand nature that is most admirable and to be held in awe. Science is an intellectual pursuit to reach beyond technology to the scientific principles that explain it. Yet science is not independent action of lone individuals but a collective activity, the work of a community of scholars who challenge, check and build upon each other's endeavors. It requires the synergistic working with others. One must persevere in self yet recognize the functioning of others. One must live a life of independence yet recognize that working with others to be beneficial.

Humans have reason, logic, knowledge and purpose. Humans have created the sciences. We have the ability to understand the natural world. We use the sciences to make sense of the world we live in. Through those sciences we have clearly established our place on this Earth. We attempt to transform it to our advantage. We know Earth revolves around the Sun. We know surrounding us is an unbelievable vast universe that is inexplicably expanding with time.

The sciences continue to address the same age-old questions that have haunted mankind through the ages. We seek answers to origins and endings. We have questions about the stars, the heavens and their meanings. We need to know who we are. We need to know how we got here and are we alone. It is the sciences that hold the methods for improving our standard of living, of knowing. It is science that more than ever gives us more time for leisure and happiness. But first and foremost we look to science to speak to those issues that we have yet to explain. Science is more than just knowledge of the natural world; it is a view of life and defines the way we live. It is the collective aspirations of our species to view a world filled with mystery, fear and wonder.

There are amazing scientific advances in genomics. Humans cannot transform nature but we can transform ourselves. Humans can change the way we think and feel. There are seven billion of us on this planet each with a unique genetic makeup. Each with an irreducible individual history. Each irreplaceable and valuable but vulnerable as well.

Science has become a part of what it means to be alive. It is the search for answers, for companionship, for love and caring for others. Science probes deeply into the psychic looking for the basics that form human feelings and emotions. Science is our longing for a better life. It is our search for order and control as well as our wonder and fear of the immensity of the cosmos. A cosmos that is indifferent to human concerns. A cosmos whose blind arbitrary natural processes we call evolution has created humans. But in reality we go about our daily life in a process of deliberating and agonizing. Everything seems to be a decision and then a second guessing. We act on many things all day long only to be unsatisfied with what we did. Even in our sleep we beguile ourselves with nightmares.

Thinking is to obtain knowledge of nature and to realize a oneness with it. To think is an act of choice, of free will. Man is a being of volitional consciousness. Reason and logic does not work automatically. For any being it is more than "To be or not to be" it is "To think or not to think." And to think we arrive at a will to live, a joy to live, a want to live, a desire to continue, hoping not to die. Thinking is that which makes me and you strive for a better life. The brain is an advanced evolutionary mechanism created to enhance and perpetuate intelligent life. I know I'm being repetitious and tiring but I can't over emphasize how logic, rational, and knowledge is important to not only staying alive but to live a good life. I intend to always return to the topic of how valuable I regard my life and that of others. When I believe something as real as life is true, words just don't seem to be enough to match the gratitude for the gift of life. No matter how many different angles you view life from; it comes out to be marvelous. I intend to keep turning this issue of life over and over in my mind. I will keep putting it into words until I get it right and it is fully understood.

≈

CRUISING AND FINDING THE FOUNDING FATHERS

When one goes ocean cruising no telling what one may find. Who knows maybe a new adventure, a different opinion, a change of venue or a change of one's mind. On a cruise there is wind in your face, sun on your back and with time to think, many thoughts sail by.

As the waves crest with white caps, each trough dips to a turquoise blue calm. Above the churning seas and below the wispy clouds ones reverie may be found. With thoughts true to world-wide beacons and within the navigational buoys the voyager's feelings, emotions and life's GPS positioning drifted about looking for truths.

In such a reverie the Founding Fathers of our great nation fixed upon the cruising voyager beacons. As the voyager settled back on a vessel built for comfort and ease, he was surprised to hear their incoming whispers on the breeze Whispers from men and women now long gone. They were the sages of wisdom who founded our country. Those men and women who made America came to join this sail with a current if not a modern look at America today. Thinking aloud, the voyager, but speculated to self, what do these great people see as a modern view?

The thought produced the unspoken question "My good men and ladies, what do you see"? The Founding Fathers responded with voices that were but soft whispers forming into responses of keen judgments on America of today.

We see big government that makes citizens small and more than feel small, to be treated small. Government is now so far away, so distant from today's citizens and further still from the individuals who made America.

The voyager thinks "Are we not true today to what you envisioned?

A whispered response. *"We see today a nation that has attained greatness through creativity, inventiveness, originality and unleashed the incentive to create wealth. This was indeed our ancestral dream. But why, pray tell, is that dream under siege today"?*

"Is America in systemic decline?"

"Absolutely not! The U.S. is the most economically dynamic and the most militarily powerful nation in the world and yet it is the most benign of all the great powers of history. You see, it is the American advantage in its can-do approach to life. Americans always believed a problem can be solved. It is an entrepreneurial culture that sees both risk and failure as natural and necessary for success. It is a mindset which came up with the internet, Microsoft and Bill Gates, Apple and Steve Jobs, Dell and more. For the next two to three decades it will remain the sole superpower. No major issue of world peace and stability can be resolved without U.S. leadership. You must however renew the efforts and work even harder to apply and extend the insights of America's founding generation. We fear and sense a decline".

"What threatens America"?

"Terrorism, drugs, violent crime, laziness, irresponsibility, in sum it is a lack of morals and the breakdown of civil society. What is most worrisome is the mass entertainment edifice that is destabilizing and injurious to the national character. It is also sad to know that you have developed into a litigation nation. Seems to us there is too much regulation which makes it harder to do business and more difficult to seek peace and simplicity in life the rule of law has become the rule of lawyers. And then there are areas today unfamiliar to us, like cronyism and the creation of complex and cumbersome legislation some of 800 pages, 2000 pages which create so many rules, studies and untold reporting and recordings. Our Mr. Jefferson penned the Preamble with but 52 precise words. Something is not right here; all this can't be good; and the situation is worsening".

"What does it take to be of value"?

"There is little limit to what a person can accomplish if government would

stay out of the way. America's culture has sustained it from the start with its creativity and hardiness, its political and economic traditions. America must continue to invite in the most hard-working and most gifted in the world. Keep immigration up but keep the nation culture firm".

"What about the needy?"

"There are always people who require help. But addressing their needs must be done in a way that does not kill incentive. The thinking that hardship and failure is due to flaws in the economic system is wrong. Charity has become entitlement and the stigma of living on charity has disappeared. That is not good. It is so because elected representatives have used the tactic of entitlement to give higher benefits to a current generation of voters for their votes. The result has been deficits and dangerously high public debt".

"What does your wisdom suggest"?

"Bear in mind that the U.S. was founded on a set of beliefs and convictions that self-evident truths of life, liberty and the pursuit of happiness should always be endorsed and embraced. Let the Preamble guide, the Constitution be the light shining on the correct path, the Bill of Rights (your present-day Amendments) be carefully modernized. Instead of seeing problems, look for opportunities. It is necessary at the same time to preserve individual liberty and national virtue. Change must be managed wisely. Above all endorse and embrace the values established at the founding".

"What would you do differently or better"?

"We gave it our all but we knew we couldn't do it all. Too few today realize the crisis-driven nature that we endured with the Declaration of In-

dependence. One must remember we were a pioneer province on the other side of an ocean. We were far removed from centers of learning and culture in London and Paris. We put on the line our very life, our fortunes, our sacred honor. We were challenging the King and his mighty seasoned army and his worldwide navy. England was the most powerful military and economic power in the world, We were challenging our own ancestry. Only those blessed with the uncommon conviction about the direction of humanity and the inalienable rights due every man could survive the task. It was an all-or-nothing moment. We were well aware of our limitations and had to put priority on what and which ideals and battles to be fought. But to answer your question we left undone some important issues. There were three of major concern that we left to future generations with the hope that the Preamble and the Constitution would enable and guide to a favorable outcome. Two of the problems it seems you adequately handled although you took an inordinate amount of time, in fact decades, to address. With the third you failed miserably and only worsened with time. That one was the Native American issue that until today remains a blight on the soul of America. Only with the death of the Native American culture did that problem diminish.

One of the undone issues was that of slavery and the Black American. You took long in solving and even longer in execution. The major effort may now be done. The right path has been laid but the cards of race continue to be shuffled and remain unsettled. Both side on this issue remain polar with significant disruption and blame on both sides.

And then there was the Women's rights issue. Women were always treated and regarded with high respect in our society but there was not enough of a recognition that they were indeed human equals. It took a century to formalize and recognize this equality ideal. This view of ideal is problematic for you see, we humans are actually very unequal at birth – Male/ Female but the most obvious.

More on the Native American issue which we cringe to discuss. Our Indian Affairs program was blatant and poorly thought out. We waged war on them. Proclaimed unilateral treaties to which they had little input and then we disregarded the terms both covertly and overtly. We treated them worse than Black Americans. We and you didn't treat them as slaves because we wanted them gone. We decimated their numbers and destroyed their villages. We wanted their land and did everything to eliminate their very essence. The Native American valued open space and never claimed ownership to land. They indeed protected the natural bounty of America but shared and did not lay private or individual claim to property. A pioneer on the other hand coveted the land to himself and to the exclusion of all others including any peers. Even today, no apologies – so few the tears of loss. Manifest Destiny took us from ocean to ocean with a wash of Native American culture".

Now most will read this vicarious exchange with the Founding Fathers and think" Oh! Just the musings of an old man on a sea cruise with nothing to do but laze about"

But think again.

Finding our Founding Fathers and listening to their advice is well worth the time, anytime.

ESSAYS

AMERICAN LAD....214
THE POWER OF TWO....215
CREATION....218
MANKIND....219
HELL....221
THEREFORE....223
CHASING MORALS....223
NATURE....225
IS TRUTH RELATIVE?....226
RAMBLING FEVER ON EMOTIONS & FEELINGS....227
DIGNITY....230
TO KNOW....232
TAKE A CHANCE ON TRUTH....234
WHAT MATTERS....235
LIFE?....235
MATTER....237
AULD LANG SYNE....238
CARPE DIEM....240
UNIQUE BEINGS....241
WEANING....243
OPINION:....243
DEFINING NATURE AND THE UNIVERSE....245
THE PHYSICAL UNIVERSE AND ME....246
NATURE AND THE REGULAR GUY....250
THE CHOSEN SPECIES....252
THE UNIVERSE AND HUMANKIND....257
THE UNIVERSE - WHY SO LARGE....258
VOID VACUUM AND SPACE....260
KNOWLEDGE AND WONDER....261
THE VERY SMALL....263

INNER SANCTUM 265
WRITING 265
ANSWERS 267
TO WRITE OR NOT TO WRITE 268
OLD LOVE LETTERS 271
MANKIND NEEDS A NEW PARADIGM 272
AWE 273
VOLITION 274
WHY ARE WE HERE 275
IS MODERN MAN REALLY CIVILIZED? 276
PRECIOUS NON-SCENTS 277
FLAVORS OF IGNORANCE 279
THREE WISHES 280
RETIRED AND THE AMERICAN CHARACTER 283
IN DEFENSE OF MARRIAGE 285
IN DEFENSE OF GENTLEMEN 288
RED LIGHTS & PORNOGRAPHY & SEXUAL CONFLICTS .... 290.
PADDLING 297
MODERN DAY POLITICS 299
THE LOST GOLDEN OPPORTUNITY 300
A MODEST VOTING PROPOSAL 302
FAITH 302
SEARCH 303
FAITH AND UNDERSTANDING 305
HATRED 310
THE DEVIL WITHIN 311
IMPRINTED 312
AN ARABIAN AFFAIR 312
THE AMERICAN TRAPPER 317

≈

ESSAYS

Essays too often come from a single-track mind.

A point of view sharpened to one's perfect position.

Ignoring whatever twist or bend it took along the way to hone the point.

Of course, the opinion must be substantiated by cleverly ignoring opposition data along the way.

How can one be forceful and convincing by allowing the seed of doubt?

Don Erdek

AMERICAN LAD

Grandparents spoke only a foreign tongue.
Parents were bilingual.
The American lad speaks American.

Grandparents could sign their names.
Parents could read and write.
The American lad has cyberspace.

Grandparents worked coal mines in Pennsylvania.
Parents worked the factories of New Jersey.
The American lad has a career that spans the globe.

Grandparents depended on candles and coal stoves.
Parents used light bulbs and furnaces.
The American lad has HVAC.

Grandparents wore woolens of drab.
Parents dressed with cotton of khaki and blue.
The American lad dons synthetics that are soft, casual and colorful.

Grandparents walked.
Parents drove.

The American lad flies.

Grandparents ate cabbage and potatoes.

Parents ate meat.

The American lad enjoys cuisine.

Grandparents toiled and died poor.

Parents worked hard and progressed.

The American lad has a profession and prospers.

THE POWER OF TWO

Boys have penises and girls have vaginas.

Could it be that:

God made little boys of string; he had a little left over so he left the thing.

Then:

God made little girls of lace; he didn't have enough so he left the space.

Did the Creator not know how to make the perfect one being?

Or was it intended to create a distinctive and unambiguous difference?

The difference itself being set as the ideal devise for the supreme plan.

So early after the creation of life there came that maximal divide.

Sex a magnificent idea, a fundamental difference.

Two sexes with complementary assets that fraternize at the crux.

The power of two.

The magic of the binary.

The unexpected glory of difference.

The synergism hidden in inequality.

Fornication at its best.

Better than all the rest.

Evolution's ultimate test.

Extending all the way back to the eukaryote and the zygote.

The very onset of sexual persuasion.

There is pair bonding in the most ancient of creatures.

Birds the descendants of 200MM year Jurassic Age creatures.

Turtle doves the deepest of attachment.

No need for preacher, shotgun, or complex social structure to legitimize sex.

The cardinal crimson red with regal crown, his mate so differently feathered in drab brown.

The silverback twice the size of his mate.

Differences determined through a binary option by nature for evolutionary reasons alone.

The most natural of facts.

The most basic of division.

The most natural of union.

The joining of male and female.

Never a duplicate; always a difference.

Sometimes a backup but never the same.

No two are clones, each to itself like no other.

The primary of difference being that of sex.

The best results come about by joining two to create a unique of one.

No one identical by the magic of the binary.

Don't tinker with diversity, for the path leads to destiny.

Sex the binary reproductive evolution is the design, part of the plan, destiny the goal.

The value is in difference.

The difference continues in creation design.

≈

Don Erdek

CREATION

Creation is the process we call God.
God is not a person, place or thing.
God is everything that has been created.

Even that which has been destroyed.
Creation is the supreme being.
Look at that which is around to find truth.

Truth is found:
In the whisper of the winds,
The babble of a brook,
The crack of thunder,
The patter of rain on a roof.

The feel of dirt between the toes,
The fragrance of a frangipani beneath one's nose,
The warmth of the sun upon one's skin,
The pull of the moon on the oceans of the world.

Grasping truths is the surest help in the time of need.
Found in the awesomeness of a night sky,
The colors of the rainbow,

As simple and as truthful as your own birth.

In the beating of your heart.

Proven with each breath taken.

God is Creation.

Creation is God.

God is not a person, place or thing.

God exists in unity with all Creation...not separate from it.

≈

MANKIND

In the big scheme of things mankind is insignificant.

In the big scheme of things mankind is magnificent.

The first statement is painfully true.

The second but a fervent hope.

Man, anthropomorphic man, with beliefs from flat earth to backs of tortoises all the way down.

Man must be the center of all things; God made it so.

Stories like the Garden of Eden, as a genesis, fit with the apple tree of knowledge.

But why were we made so tiny, so small, so limited in real estate?

Why so stingy when he made so much more out there?

In the big scheme of things man has hardly a chance with so much space.

Just why pray tell make it that way?

A bit more dirt, a bit more space, maybe a bit more to share.

Then again let us not challenge the scheme; he gave us a brain to figure it all out and loaded that with dreams.

Make the most of it he hastened to say.

Follow my words...I'll show you the way,

AH! the words, so many words from so many different men.

All professing to have heard the word.

Might the words not have been spoken, but instead is constantly being shown?

Just look around both near and distant star.

For true truth is not that far.

Given a body and the senses is all that is needed to be significant.

Add a brain and a conscience to become magnificent.

≈

HELL

Hell is a cruel and oppressive place.
Sinners suffer unspeakable torments.
Endless suffering for all eternity.

Sins committed during a mortal life.
Terrible fate awaits.
Fire, brimstone, pain to the devil's glee.

Souls that lived an unjust life.
The afterlife unbearable.
Such a scare.

Avoid the tilt of God's wrath.
Favor his mercy.
After life in heaven to be sought.
Fear of hell a cornerstone of doctrine.

The fear of hell helps lead souls to heaven.
Be a believer.
Avoid sinful behavior.
Embrace the virtuous life.

Hell remains a powerful concept.

Religion appropriates this literature of suffering.

Eternal damnation to the disbeliever.

Hell a deterrent to sinful behavior.

Sins themselves skillfully defined.

Few believe they will end there even though not many of us are saintly.

Hell provides a satisfaction that the sinful get just desert.

Include the non-believer for his boldness.

All will be corrected.

Gone somewhere in limbo.

A threshold away from hell to save un-baptized babies.

Purgatory remains a safety valve if but one repents.

Has hell outlived its usefulness?

Will we humans ever mature?

Probably not!

Hell remains a frightening deterrent to sinfulness.

Don't count on humans to be civil.

Expect not justice to be served.

At least not here on Earth in real time.

THEREFORE

The sun rises in the morning and sets in the evening.
That is real wherever you may be.

You were born of a woman and sired by a man.
That is real whoever you may be.

You need to breathe and you need to eat.
That is real if you hope to exist.
You need to think.
You need to act.
That is if you seek to persist.

There was a genesis.
There has to be a purpose.
There must be a destiny.

Genesis how-ever, when-ever, why-ever is truth.
The will to live, the shun of dying, is the key to purpose.
Awareness, the desire to know, is the path to destiny.

≈

CHASING MORALS

The world is imperfect; always will be.

Humankind is a sorry lot; cracks run through it.

Civilization is not yet ready to be weaned of war.

Religions cleave rather than unite; they claim to, but they don't.

We are all vulnerable.

Anything can happen at any time.

We have need to understand human vulnerability.

We have to recognize human frailty.

Don't we see and witness human weakness every day?

Those moments from small disappointments to blows that bring us to our knees.

Life's experiences should make for a better life...better things.

Yet it seems that humans are born without a hard wire for morality.

It is the software and apps of maturation that develop conscience.

Better things come at a price.

We yield our freedoms and free-will to rule of law.

Rules and laws must not be cast that impede human ingenuity and genius.

Allow individuals to be their best, do their best.

Greater effort to guide conscience to a higher level of good for self and others.

We are all individuals.

Life sustaining actions are carried out by self with little help from any other.

We breathe without thought whether awake, asleep or comatose.

Our heart beats, the blood flows, with the self ever correcting a rate.

Digestion occurs under unthinking control.

Sense perception and reason can give us knowledge of the physical world.

What must happen is to allow the best to do their best.

Every other individual must strive to be the best they can be.

Rules and laws must not be cast that impede that effort.

Greater effort guides a conscience to a higher level of good to self and for others.

The superior realm of the inner sanctum must be pursued.

Once beyond the basic requirements of persevering can a higher level of human existence be entertained.

Only then on to what is good and what is bad.

Making life a fulfilling value by just doing proper.

≈

NATURE

Man is part of nature...a small part.

All that man possesses whether mental or physical, are entirely and solely within nature's province.

To know ourselves we need to know as much as we can about nature.

Human beings are a part of nature as any other thing and do not in any way inhabit or occupy some separate space on this planet or elsewhere in the universe.

Humans are not exempt from the laws of nature that govern the entire universe and all of nature's events.

A thorough understanding of nature and its ways is the highest form of knowledge available to humans.

To most humans this is a too difficult a task.

Indeed a difficulty that within humanity is rare.

≈

IS TRUTH RELATIVE?

Finding truth an impossible task.

In the world today everything is relative.

You have your truth; I have mine.

Purposeful conversation dies on the vine.

Harmful is this thinking that everything is relative.

Leading to the conclusion there is no need to seek truth.

No good, no evil; all an individual's point of view.

Changing circumstances, past history, one's own desires propel each through life.

These desires, those experiences are personal.

Nothing else...no one else matters.

Truth is in denial lest certain feelings, certain ideas, might harmfully be challenged.

No one wants to be told they are wrong.

Political correctness carries the day.

Easier not to hurt feelings by saying all is relative.

Smooth feathers; stroke the hair; preen the ego.

Don't challenge another's belief.

It is this pernicious thinking that persists today.

Abandoning truth creates confusion.

Confusion leads to chaos.

America is in denial.

The human race is cracking.

Apocalypse is coming down.

≈

RAMBLING FEVER ON EMOTIONS AND FEELINGS

Another pursuit.

To identify the feeling of respect.

The Fifth commandment...honor thy mother and thy father.

Should be respect instead of honor.

There is a distinct difference between an emotion and a feeling.

That which are exhibited by tears and sadness in the face is something others can see but is only a small portion of the feelings felt inside.

Emotions and feelings are generally assume to be the same.

They are not!

Emotions are external signs that others can see.

Others interpret these as being what is felt inside.

But others can't really know what is inside.

Others may merely gauge.

Thus emotions are but a reflection of the inner strife of the true feelings.

This has turned to questions on hatred.

What is that inside feeling of hatred as distinct from the emotional signs of detest?

Think but of the stink-eye of a Saudi mullah.

Then there is yet another feeling that is of concern.

That is respect.

Why is honoring of another an important emotion when it is respect of that person which means so much more.

Honor is an emotion...respect a feeling.

Which leads back to the Fifth Commandment..."Honor thy mother and thy father".

I do believe "Respect thy mother and father" so much more profound.

I wonder does the bible distinguish between emotions and feelings or does it treat them as same?

Now what might I be thinking

Really it is much more direct then one may assume.

I am not questioning any religious belief, the bible, or the 5th commandment.

I am trying to understand the difference between emotions and feelings.

Thus also comes the question of hatred (a negative feeling) and respect (a positive feeling).

What I ask is the faith-based opinion of hatred...merely a sin?

Why does one hate?

Do we respect out of fear?

Does respect come from soul or conscience and if so does hate also?

So where is all of this going?

It leads to the question of how much are we lead through life by feelings and emotions and not by logic and rational.

If we think before we act we will most likely be making a wise choice.

Alternately if we only use feelings or emotions to direct our actions hell knows what may happen.

Others viewing our action can understand them if we use logic but can only surmise if we act from feelings.

≈

DIGNITY

Life, liberty and the pursuit of happiness.

So what is pursuit of happiness?

How can it be defined?

How does one recognize it when achieved?

What is enduring happiness?

Personal happiness can be defined best by one word - dignity.

We should all seek dignity.

Dignity must be earned.

We each need to learn how to earn dignity.

Earn dignity by being responsible for self.

Strive to live life on one's own terms.

Do not lose dignity by expecting something from someone else.

Above all do not lose dignity by depending on a government to provide for dignity.

Ones dignity resides in oneself and namely in one's own life and one's own health.

Dignity is your life.

It is how you maintain your health and wealth.

Your life, your health, your livelihood is your responsibility to yourself.

You should work for your own home.

You should provide for your own food.

You should clothe yourself.

You should maintain your health in youth and old age.

Being responsible is your dignity.

Do not entertain the thought or voice the phrases "someone is not doing enough for me" or "I deserve".

Do not sign on with laws by the government where-in it is expected that the government do more for me or my health.

Plan on living a good healthy life guided by responsible.

Work with self-reliance so as to earn dignity.

Protect your dignity and let no one take it from you.

Expect the government to provide only protection for the right to live and one's property rights.

It is up to the government to protect us but do not let it provide for us or create our dignity.

Now if for some reason one is not able to accomplish these life goals then family, friends, community and religion need step up.

In that order they best are able to help in ways where one loses as little dignity as possible.

Only after all options are gone should one expect government to assist.

Even then it is not politicians who provide the help; it is others who pay taxes that do.

Remember everything in life comes at a price.

We are paid to do a job.

We in turn pay for food, housing, clothing and our needs and wants.

But dignity has no price.

It cannot be bought or sold.

Indeed to precious to give away.

My dignity, your dignity is ours to have and to hold.

To cherish or not.

To work for or not.

To expect something from others or not.

≈

TO KNOW

In the timeless Universe there spins a globe.

On its crust sit those tiny beings called people.

They deal not with the vastness of space but concentrate on the smallness of home.

These peoples are shackled to the thin veneer of their crusty place.

So plain to see, so small and limited they be.

So insignificant is the expanse of their providence.

So foolish their vision it all be for themselves.

How limited the reach to the vastness they know to be way beyond.

Created over the eons as the remnants and scattering of supernova.

Life has become an exceptional association of carbon and minerals and water.

Death is feared or welcomed as a return to non-biological origin.

However there-in lies the magnificence of the peoples --- their knowing.

Knowing that they are aware of it all.

Knowing they have indeed been created and have evolved on this planet Earth.

Knowing the body, the brain, may be made of dirt and air and water but the mind senses it all.

All the way back from here to there where the micro-static remains.

All this time, all this space, all that matters has its place.

The Universe has evolved, is still evolving, and carries along the human race.

Sometimes fast, other times slow, but inevitably at a steady pace.

It is that pace and purpose that must be addressed.

To that purpose the peoples must acquiesce.

Dust, dirt, ash, air, water ...the boundaries on either side of brilliance.

≈

TAKE A CHANCE ON TRUTH

Truth not hard to find.

It passes easily into an open mind.

Close not the senses' clues.

They do not lie, seldom confuse.

Trust what is real around you.

The senses are instruments inborn.

Given to each as gifts of Genesis.

The keys to open the pearly gates the spiritual tries to hide.

Truths for you to find.

Trust in innate senses a path to unwind.

≈

WHAT MATTERS

So much taken for granted.

Life is good.

Life is real.

Life is what each of us truly have.

So what can be the greatest, grandest, most magnificent matter in the entire universe?

≈

LIFE?

Well kind of.

DNA is life.

But there is life in so many creatures and forms.

Possibly life exists in other quarters in the greater everything.

SCIENCE AND TECHNOLOGY?

Well sure they make life easier and longer.

KNOWLEDGE?

Knowing that there is a Universe with its Big Bang, Black Holes, Neutrinos and Quarks.

RELIGION?

Well it could be if not distorted by axioms, compliance, organizations and practices.

AWARENESS?

Knowing that you know.

Knowing that 14.2 billion years is the age of the Universe.

Knowing the billions of galaxies, the expansion of time and space and Einstein's E= MC2.

Knowing Earth in its magnificence.

We know so much.

How much more yet to know.

So much that matters is taken for granted.

The question becomes "So what really matters?".

There is matter everywhere - near and far.

Matter composes the planets and the sun.

Matter is in the stars, the galaxies, the cosmos.

The whole of the universe itself is matter.

Each of us is composed of matter.

The magnificence is that we are matter that knows all other matter and everything that matters or so we think.

≈

MATTER

Life matters.
We are made of matter.
We are what matters most.

There is indeed in each of us the will to matter.
Or does the will to believe matter more?
Could the will to live be the key to make things matters, and might that be what matters most?

It is the time we live and how we live, that should carry the most weight.
Yet many, so many, who came in the ages before no longer matter.
So why should I? So why should you? Of what significance might you and I be?

Well now, maybe, the here and now is an important answer to the matter?
With a full belly and being in a safe abode one needs to define its lot among the stars.
Find the sense of your life and what it's all about.

We live in an age of unprecedented ambition and restlessness.
We search for a religion and hunger for redemption.

But are we not, living in a golden age of knowledge?
An age of freedom, liberty, individual ability, and curiosity.
An unfettered life of health, wealth, and ambition.
Not even the richest of past kings and queens had what we have.
There should not be a battle or even a search for mortality...that is just not the way nature says it to be.
Finding that sense to life and what it's about is our best fit.
We need to live fully and vibrantly in the present.
How to do that is absolutely and indubitably up to you.

The universe and nature and the creator are all one.
That one, that omnipotence, found fit to form energetic matter that thinks and is aware.

Over endless time it formed a combination of matter which should be made to matter.
That is what made me; that is what made you.
Might that be the "evermore" or so be it "forevermore" in the same state as was before.

≈

AULD LANG SYNE

Change need not be something new.

Better to cherish that in my hand, than want what is not.

Love the comfort of a broken-in shoe.

Wax the old wheels, they still don't wobble.

Dust the TV, it's not the picture, but my eyes that matter.

So what's the message?

What's my point?

Hold on to the now, that's the point!

Pull up the reins on that progressive effort to change.

Change just because things are not good enough?

What's so poor about the now?

What's so poor about the past?

Is what we have so poor that we should discard as trash?

Should those we know and love be forgotten and not thought of?

Should old times past and lessons learned be ignored?

Should "Auld Lang Syne" be our daily song?

"Should auld acquaintances be forgot and never brought to mind?"

"Should auld acquaintances be forgot, and days of auld lang syne?"

We should retain and conserve old times and old friends.

We should toast them now and always.

We should keep them close and not liberate them into the trash bins of change.

What can be more pleasant than our family and friends?

What can be better than that long-ago new-born now loved more than ever?

So be it with the Constitution.

So be it with the many freedoms we now enjoy.

Wisdom will show that bigger government and rash progressiveness invokes trash before the change.

What is better than to live in America?

Even those who claim they will leave if they don't get their way - don't,. They stay!

What could be better than our Constitution?

Give it pause, give it thought, but only carefully ever so carefully, evoke change.

What could be better than the freedoms we now have?

Indeed we are in confusing times when difficult to distinguish
between "add to" or "take away".

Life's lessons showed us how to depend upon our self.

Showed us how each, not some other, can make things better.

Better - rather than, depending on some other.

Or simply discarding for something new.

So many years now we have chosen poorly.

From the decade ago "hope" and "change".

To present day polar disruptions.

Our decision-makers are deeply flawed.

We, ourselves, have become close-minded, rigid, stiff, unbending.

Collectively we have disabled freedom system.

Shame on us all!

≈

CARPE DIEM

It would be wonderful if we had ready answers.
Take those moments when asking "Why".

Seize the day I believe to be an intelligent course.
Add awareness to the mix, stir in a hint of curiosity.

Prize what emerges.
Cull by the desire to do better.
They look the same but aren't.

Rest assured answers can be found.
Choose wisely.
Truth and fiction are dressed with similar words.

≈

UNIQUE BEINGS

Every human life involves an unfathomable mystery.

Man is the riddle of the Universe.

Endowed with an awareness of oneself.

Mind, memory, affection and purposefulness centered in an ego.

Conscious of oneself.

Entrusted with a mysterious endowment to make the most of a unexplained life.

Possessing an exceptional ability to project a purpose into the future and head toward it.

Gifted with affection, living in other lives more than in one's own, albeit recondite because it is common.

Conscious planning causing changes.

In the realm of inanimate nature change comes by pressure and coercion from beyond.

The sun makes planets keep their course.

The moon causes the tides to rise.

Gravitation forces rivers to run.

The chemistry of soil and sunshine drive the trees to grow.

In personal life a different process emerges.

Here the most significant changes are consciously chosen purposes projected ahead.

One is not so much forced from behind as drawn before, not so much pushed as pulled.

The stars are not so strange as the mind that studies them.

Electrons and protons present no enigma as the ability of man to remember and hope.

With this mysterious endowment each of us has been entrusted.

To make the most of it our primary task.

Yet, even in the realm of organized knowledge, we know more about the stars than ourselves.

We take a more objective view of heavenly bodies than we do of our own mind.

Is it man's strange penchant to confront last what lies nearest?

Wrestling with every conceivable factor involved with the human situation,

Before one faces the primary task - oneself!

WEANING

Mankind is not yet ready to be weaned of:

- ✓ War.
- ✓ Religion and superstition.
- ✓ Nationalism and Tribalism.
- ✓ Capitalism.
- ✓ Misplaced hero worship.
- ✓ Hate.

Mankind must seek true value in:

- Virtue
- Knowledge.
- Wisdom.
- Justice.
- Trust.
- Freedom.
- Liberty

≈

OPINION:

Humans spend almost all of their life seeking pleasure and avoiding pain.

Now we can understand why there is an avoidance of pain.

But why so much time spent in seeking pleasure with too little time for getting smart.

For most, the end of a formal education is an end and not a commencement.

Only one percent of humans pursue knowledge; ninety-nine percent opt for ignorance.

All rue Alzheimer's but most daily allow the brain to slowly atrophy.

Selfie's, Dr. Pepper, potato chips, CSI, Duck Dynasty are top priority.

Lots of time is locked in for text messaging, virtual reality, and video games.

Lots of time for nonsense; learning something of value is not what most want to do.

Most eighteen-year olds have an attitude that they already have all the smarts needed for life.

Those in the twenties have fashion and clothes and so many cute and charming things to do.

By the thirties full blast and living for today.

The forties slip fast with no time to think.

The fifties are gone before you blink.

And by the time you get to seventy you are dumber than dog-poop and smell about the same.

Well you get the picture...living is too busy for learning other than by default.

Yeah...yeah...yeah...I know what is said about opinions.

Everyone has one...they are like a**-holes no one needs a second.

So if you read this far, you've heard mine and I don't need to hear yours.

DEFINING NATURE AND THE UNIVERSE

The Universe is all that physically exists.

By definition it is the entire, the whole.

Humankind reside in and is a part of the Universe.

The Universe becomes the whole body of human knowledge of things and phenomena known or postulated.

The Universe expands when humankind's knowledge of the things and phenomena expand.

The Universe are those things that humans know as well as those things humans have yet to uncover.

So the definition of the Universe is given by the knowledge and duration of human existence and human awareness.

The Universe is part of Nature.

Nature is more than the Universe and therefore more than humans know.

Nature is more than humans have yet to discover or uncover.

Nature encompasses the known, the unknown, and the unknowable.

Nature acts infinitely and in infinite ways.

Humankind need to accept that by their own physical limitations there are things of Nature forever unknowable.

*Nature as defined by Webster states that Nature is to be born and is the inherent character of a person or thing.

**NATURE as stated above is infinitely more and is personified as what humans identify as infinity.

≈

THE PHYSICAL UNIVERSE AND ME

The universe is a single, unique, speed of light expanse that is necessary for human existence.

The universe created our sun, the planets and the blue sea earth particularly for humans...or so we think.

The universe neither commands nor judges our existence but mandates that we live in all respect to its natural laws.

The search and understanding of natural laws increases our chance for survival and continued existence as one of nature's creatures.

To date and for all intents and purposes we are unique, and the most magnificent of creation.

Everything we know or can know is found in the universe which includes all matter, energy, and forces.

And we, humankind, are composed of matter and move and exist with compliance to universal laws.

From this I seek to define the simple one and only "me."

The "what," the "where," the "when" the "how," and lastly, the "why."

The "what" is the me.

We are made of matter and move with force and energy.

In this respect we have no differences and only kinship with the entire physical universe.

Even thinking is a physical thing that exists in the human brain.

It comprises neurons and synapses and paths of connection known as memory.

Alike, yet also different and more complex than a hard-wired computer.

We may believe that personal identity is an abstract thing...it is not.

In its simplest form it become "me and not you."

That is the distinction between one's own self and all others.

This evokes a barrage of feelings and emotions to identify and isolate oneself from all others.

My computer is different than yours.

One cares about oneself simply because a person is committed, immediately and unthinkingly to survival and flourishing in the body and mind that he or she is.

One pursues one's life....it is the endeavor to persevere.

One doesn't need a reason to pursue it.

It is absurd to ask why we should care for our self.

Then comes the "where."

The universe is the "where."

All the mass, the energy, and the forces make up the universe.

The universe is our physical realm; it is what constitutes and creates our reality.

The speed of light and gravity are absolutes we are constrained to live by.

The universe has a finite age of some 14.2 billion years.

The speed of light is also a finite barrier at 186,000 miles per second.

This combination by simple extension creates a barrier to how much we can know of the cosmos.

In layman's terms the big bang created all there is 14.2 billion years ago.

Whether this is an exact or final number is irrelevant; it probably will change.

So the "when" becomes today the time in years after the creation of the universe some 14.2 billion years ago.

Our "when", because of time's arrow, is in constant movement... yesterday...today... tomorrow.

However and inexplicably, it moves in one direction only...older.

This unidirectional movement is the way it is in this physical universe of humankind.

We need to accept it as an absolute of the physics of humanity.

Now to the "how."

This is perhaps the simplest of questions.

You were born of a woman; sired by a man.

This is real whoever you may be.

There was an immensity of time before without the me.

There was a linage of others who persisted along the passageway of human creation.

A great and wonderful line of humanity specific to the me of today.

We must grasp as unquestionably true an acceptance and an open realization that one's life is intimately, inexplicably, and inextricably tied to ones parents and ancestors and they to the universe that begot them.

The open realization that one's body, one's mind, one's life is all there is and must be all that one needs.

The "why"... the philosopher stone of questions.

The "why" is an enigma.

Let me say what I know.

I know I don't know how to explain the "why" by appealing to anything in the physical universe.

The "why" needs definition to be sought in that outside the physical universe.

As all of us know there is a spiritual universe.

The universe is metaphysical...beyond the physics of time and space.

So the "why" remains an enigma?

But that doesn't mean it is beyond human questioning.

We start with our assets, the known, and add to the known as we search for yet to be found parts of the physical universe.

Add to this mankind's prime forte...awareness and curiosity.

This is something no hard-wired computer has.

So we must pursue the "why are we here" as vigorously as we seek knowledge of the physical universe.

Curiosity and awareness is an elevation of the soul.

"The spiritual universe" is a subject, a topic, a puzzle, a riddle beyond all riddles.

Whence mankind sought answers in a creed, or a religion to solve the mystery.

To most, belief in a religion is the final solution to the mystery.

To some, curiosity and awareness keeps the mystery of the spiritual universe as an open topic.

≈

NATURE AND THE REGULAR GUY

The big picture for a regular guy (gal) as classified by the main categories:

1. Universe
2. Solar system
3. Sun
4. Earth
5. Life
6. Humanity

7. Society
8. Family
9. Self

Most humans would invert this sequence and put "self" on the top.
Humanity has the persistence and insistence in being anthropomorphic.
To humans, the universe, the natural world, is incomplete without a human presence.
So how to live in a spiritual balance with the vastness, the powerful, the almighty universe;
Simple... just give it the proper reverence for the gift of life for the rest of your life.

Natalism (my word, my definition) is to be born of a time in the known universe.
It is a belief in the existence of a supreme power over shadowing all that is man.
It encompasses all there is of matter and forces.
It recognizes man's limitations to know the entirety of the universe based on man's own physical and mental limitations.
It further postulates that man will never attain complete knowledge.
It encourages man to pursue knowledge to the limit, with the awareness and curiosity, and the acknowledgement that man is not yet knowing of what his limit.

This in itself is a most peculiar perspective of man.
That reason and observation of the universe becomes that what he is embedded in.
A recognition that man is not the center of the universe.
Yet man is an entity that knows that the universe has only man to know the universe.
Or so we think! ... or yet to know!

Now what is that regular guy(gal)?
The details of the development of the regular guy(gal) is pretty straight forward.
We may question the fundamental architecture of life with the

question "is it God or Nature that created the living me".
Yet there is little doubt that an adult organism is male or female and born from a single cell.
Male sperm uniting with the female egg creates a new entity... a new person.
That it is a god like natural development we all want to agree.
But nature's hand from that point of creation to a living adult organism is the sole majesty of nature at work.

We humans, our brains, our bodies are a result of eons of evolution.
Driven by the pressures of natural selection and genetic variability we are here on earth.
Below the sun, on this side of the moon, we find the link between creature and environment an essential to keep.

Oh yes! The environment, all that is Nature, we must respect.
On bended knee and with a slight genuflect we pay homage to the world's "greenies".
Idealism a heavy cross to carry; the sweat created, crosses the brow, into the eyes, does indeed obstruct clarity of vision.

THE CHOSEN SPECIES

We are a very special species.

Perhaps the chosen species.

We, it seems, are alone among all species to have grasped the reality of the universe around us.

We see the beauty of nature.

We try to give value to our life, as well as to the sanctity of the life of another.

We attempt to extend an unbridled quality of mercy to others of our own kind.

We even seek to expand that same concern for the universe into which we were birthed.

Humanity arose on this earth through an accumulated series of events that spans millennia.

It was the history and natural possibilities afforded by this planet, around this sun, in this galaxy, In the known universe in which we were conceived and there upon matured.

Even with these given circumstances, humanity was not predestined to reach any goal except through its own endeavors.

Man was not born into a civilization...it was man who created civilized life.

Man learned to live with and control the forces of this earth...of nature.

Fire, the wheel, steel, to read, write and learn from mistakes.

Civilization...learning to live with one another.

Through the learning ages humanity answered to no power other than its own existence fortified by that individual effort to persist.

It was a wisdom based on self-understanding and the strive to continue to live that spurred us on.

This endeavor to persist has saved us in the past and will continue to save us in the future.

We have in the past, as well as today, only this meager planet to inhabit and to call home.

Through our intelligence and curiosity we realize that in addition there is a vast universe to unfold.

There-in lies the value and meaning of our personal lives and where we are going and why.

It is up to each of us to get hold of our human condition and take another step on our journey.

So what is that human condition?

The human condition is a historic one.

It is the product of not only 6 millennia of civilization, but much further back, across hundreds of millennia.

When objectively studied across its entire traverse, the history of humanity tells a story.
It provides answers to the mystery of life and becomes the key to learning how and why our species arose and survived.

The mystery is in the rocks…dust thou art; to dust return-it.

With that knowledge of natural history, human existence may be simpler than we thought.

We are made from a man and a woman.

We are individuals who are separated from a mother at birth to be independent in body and of one mind.

In life we are alone and fragile and from the start we need help, mainly from that mother and a father who care. But without a doubt each of us is a biological species adapted only to live on the biological planet called earth.

The human mind did not arrive on planet earth full blown.

Even today it lacks pure reason and emotional fulfillment.

For better or worse, our mind has been our faithful guide; and till death do us part.

Our mind attained its present form from a maze of wide and narrow paths of endless possibilities.

Each path was a result of DNA mutation and natural selection that was channeled to the best form and function for both the brain and the body sensory system.

Whether by accident or serendipity or synergism our body, brain, and genome gained its present level.

What then is needed to continue the long-term survival of our species is intelligence and self-understanding.

We must seek greater independence of thought.

More independence of thought… more even than that tolerated today in the most advanced democratic societies or the most understanding of religions.

Our choices for the future are profoundly moral ones.

Our fulfillment as the chosen species depends on knowledge and understanding both of which is still lacking.

We need to further that conscience that knows right from wrong and good from evil.

And even more so, a common decency still needs to be universally found.

To this subject of common decency, we wonder if we basically are good but become corrupt by forces of evil?

Or are we innately a beast yet redeemable by the forces of good?

Might a biological truth lie somewhere beneath what these questions are asking?

We know inside each of us are both saint and sinner, a champion of truth but hypocritical at times.

This is not because humankind has failed to reach some ideological or religious ideal but merely and simply of the way of the past and how our species originated across millions of years of biological evolution.

And so be it with frightening ease, good people do bad things...it is that beast within!

Let's be clear on this view it is not a Deity test of humanity; it is part of our nature.

Within each of us that internal conflict of good and evil will remain.

But neither it is in any shape or form a machination of Satan...destroy that myth!

It is just the way things have so far worked out.

We will eventually find the right light...the best of paths.

The modern human still has so many problems to solve.

We must find solutions for the clash of competing religions,

A way to ease the biases of nationalism,

A recognition of the ambiguities and lack of moral reasoning,

And most important to expand the value of an individual itself.

It's been a long hard road with still a far way to go.

Our choices are profoundly moral ones.

Our fulfillment of that chosen species depends upon knowledge still lacking.

Don't just bite ... eat the whole damn friggin' apple!

Look for and find a conscience that can clearly identify right from wrong. Good from evil.

Expand that search for that boundless knowledge and common decency we have yet to find.

≈

THE UNIVERSE AND HUMANKIND

Guided by the essence of creation.

The universe reveals itself as nature.

Nature is the bang that lit the stars of evolution.

Thereupon in now time and chosen space did Earth adhere.

Globs of stardust voraciously gathered.

Entropy not prevailing.

Chaos mastered.

Nature fitting bits into a helix of evolutionary mutations.

Success accepted. Weakness discarded.

The success of the ages slow but ever moving to a destiny design.

Enduring whatever the barrier.

Circumventing any obstacle.

Genes emerging ever in conflict with entropic chaos.

Ever striving, ever enduring, always pursuing.

Advancing or mutating to sidestep extermination.

The magic of humankind came later - much, much later.

In reference to nature, humankind honors with an homage to physical laws.

These laws established at the Genesis display the versatility of evolution.

And so be it.

≈

THE UNIVERSE - WHY SO LARGE

Why is the universe so large?

It is so very, very vast.

What could be the reason for that?

Even the wise say it was much "smaller" back "then".

Maybe only the size of a dime at plus one time after the bang.

Was it "size" or "time" or neither the source of creation?

Both time and size apparently started simultaneously.

Both time and size are unidirectional.

But, what pray tell, started the human race and why at such a later time and distant place?

That something is something we need to discover.

Maybe it is not a boundary; rather it is as yet an unknown.

Then again, may the human point of view be irrelevant at mega scale and endless time?

Now for us, what we think may delight us.

What we discover may be of use to us.

What is attractive or unattractive may be important to us.

None-the-less, the universe cares less and continues to carry on to its own will.

Plain speak, it is the real of the universe to show no tilt for human care.

This is a sharp strike to us as cold and inhuman.

Well, yes indeed, cold and inhuman and onto a dirty crust on a fringe sphere we are thrust.

Early on humankind found the need for significance.

A need to evaluate and place creation in this earthly garden of Eden.

An explanatory story with gravity and mystery to seek and define life existence.

The need to explain the mystic and account for disasters.

This mono-species sought a foil for its minute proportion and to placate the ravages of time.

A magic cloak was woven with invisible and imagined threads of miracles and superstition

Works well for earthlings!

Don Erdek

VOID VACUUM AND SPACE

Just what is a "void"?

Is it something or is it nothing or the absence of something and then what is it that is absent?

In addition just what is a "vacuum"?

What is "space"?

When "space" expands exactly what is it expanding into...a "void"?

If there is matter and if there is a "void" between bits of matter; is "void" something that matter is not?

And at the time of the big bang which we are told that everything was compressed into infinitesimal "space"; was "space" and matter the same?

And way back then what was it that was outside that infinitely compressed matter and "space"?

And if at the time of the big bang if only matter was compressed, then where and what was "space"?

And if "space" was infinitely small at the big bang and it's growing infinitely big now; what is it that is growing?

And if it is "space" that is growing just how does nothing grow?

Or is it just stretching; then how does nothing stretch?

I don't know if all of this matters or not.

I don't know if I'm stretching a nothing into something.

Or if I'm boring a Tibetan monk.

KNOWLEDGE AND WONDER

Some things matter; some matter not at all.

The grandest of human achievement is our scientific accomplishments.

It is our collective ability to create knowledge through the human intellect.

It is our joint effort to understand nature that is most admirable and to be held in awe.

We use the sciences to make sense of the world we live in.

Through the sciences we have clearly established our place on this earth.

We know we revolve around the sun.

We know surrounding us is an unbelievably vast universe that is inexplicably expanding with time.

In our personal life, science addresses the same age-old questions that has haunted us through the ages.

We seek answers to origins and endings.

We have questions about the stars, the heavens and their meanings.

We need to know who we are.

We need to know how we got here and are we alone.

It is science that holds the methods for improving our standard of living.

It is science that more than ever gives us more time for leisure and to a pursuit of progress and a happier life.

But first and foremost we look to science to speak to those issues that we cannot explain.

Science is more than just knowledge of the natural world.

It is a view of life and defines the way we live.

It is the collective aspiration of our species to view a world filled with mystery, fear, and wonder.

Science has become a part of what it means to be alive.

It is our search for answers, for companionship, for love and caring for others.

Science is not a God-given truth; it is our longing for a better life. It is our search for order and control and our wonder and fear at the immensity of the cosmos.

But in reality we go about our daily life in a process of deliberating and agonizing.

Everything seems to be a decision and then a second guessing.

We act on many things all day long only to regret what we did.

Even in sleep we beguile ourselves with nightmares.

Let me be so bold to present a different observation.

It may be critical and judgmental but it is a bird's eye view.

Humans are not a particularly admirable lot.

All they desire is food, sex, some creature comforts, and a modicum of security to enjoy life.

The vast majority, ninety to ninety-nine percent plus, look for little more than that.

Most humans love evil things.

They spend their lives abusing good things ...food, drugs, water, the atmosphere, the land.

And there are just too friggin many of them for this one small planet.

As for those sciences they did a lot to create gun powder, TNT, and A-bombs.

Then those same scientists create Nobel peace prizes...go figure?

I may have a birdbrain but most humans are whack-jobs!

≈

THE VERY SMALL

The universe can at times be a very confusing place.

Who and why was it made so?

The microscopic world, for example, operates in obscure and unfamiliar ways.

The human senses are unable to grasp what is going on in the ultra-small.

Might it be, the mind and senses are unable to cope for reasons we have yet to find?

We understand phenomena on the familiar everyday scale of things, what we call the real world.

But our sense fails us in the world of the ultramicroscopic.

Quantum mechanics which explains the micro world tells us that our senses are of little use.

Human senses know not, see not, and feel vague what lies beyond, what is hidden below.

When we deeply probe we become confused, our detection devices not sensitive enough.

The electron, proton, neutron, the force of gravity, a photon of light, the electromagnetic spectrum are detected only macroscopically.

The fundamental workings of the universe evade us.

Aspects of which are vastly different from our expectations.

Is it too bold of us to seek answers to deep questions?

It will require exceptional mental flexibility to find answers.

With humbleness and appreciation, we must acknowledge our limitations.

It is the skeleton key to what we seek.

Or does a spiritual voice caution not to seek?

≈

INNER SANCTUM

How often have you searched for something that was with you all along?

Those flashbacks, deja vu, on the tip of your tongue.

Remembrances you try to recall to no avail.

Until you allow a time for peaceful repose.

Sometimes thoughts and ideas emerge from an ancient swamp.

Or a boggy mass of unused facts.

Truth is they were there all along.

But deeper down and held in your inner sanctum.

Inner sanctum may be a world of quantum foam.

Where quarks and super strings intertwine.

Maybe the only place for eternal truth.

≈

WRITING

Write like you think.

You think with short thoughts.

You combine those into a sequence of thoughts.

One linked to the other.

One following the other.

The one following carries a link to the one before in some fashion as well as to the following one.

A new paragraph is created for a change in venue. to a more or lesser degree.

Writing for one's own pleasure is good.

Writing that pleases others is better.

Don't worry about what to write.

Don't seek the right words.

Record the thoughts.

There is no such thing as not having a thought.

Have you ever tried not to think, not to have a thought?

Even thinking about not thinking belie the fact...it can't be done.

We think in simple few word thoughts.

The knack is to record them as they flow.

Don't try too hard to correct or perfect a thought before writing it down.

Usually one thought forms a link to another like thought.

If we think we can write.

When we write we learn to think better.

Often as we write the words and sequence of words are formed between the thought to the tip of the pen.

Now here are a few words about my own writing.

I write for others to know me, especially my children.

I do hope one of them, if not all of them, pick up the threads of my writing and carry them onward.

My writings have messages between myself and myself whoever that may be at any one time.

These messages are mind conversations with an open channel to hear what an intimate conversation with the nature and the past that is within me... my being.

These messages believe in the value of any one life and in humanity in general; but yet with tongue in cheek about all of our short comings.

These messages are written with a looseness of epistolary style that allows me to wander wherever my thoughts take me.
Life is what it is and not what it ought to be.

≈

ANSWERS

It would be wonderful if we had ready answers.

Too often we don't.

At least not to the deepest of questions.

Those times when asked "Why?".

Carpe deim I believe to be an intelligent route.

If life is seized many paths emerge.

Direction lay out by past experience.

Put brain cells to the task.

Add awareness to the mix.

Stir in a hint of curiosity.

Then choose wisely.

Truth and fiction are dressed in similar words.

They look the same but aren't.

Rest assured among the chaos it can be found.

Not all, but enough.

≈

TO WRITE OR NOT TO WRITE

My good friend, Kenney, didn't write.

I wish he did.

I would so love to feel his presence and rethink his thoughts with a scan of his words.

No writings from my father who died when I was but one.

I wish I could read his words and know something of the man who made me.

Those letters from mom, I hold dear; all the more since she also is no longer here.

Love letters and friends' letters wrap in string or ribbons are priceless regardless of dust they gather.

All these past yellowing writings form ghostly script that still evoke strong emotions.

Just try to toss one of those old crumpled letters into a log fire and feel the tremors of a personal loss.

Written words come from the hand of one to the eyes and heart of another.

Written words are as strong as if chiseled in stone.

Those that are handwritten are recognized just from the author's unique script.

But it seems from the ways of today that penmanship and long hand soon shall be long gone.

We know the past by what was written.

We think we know what once from a mouth was spoken; but yet not certain what were the exact words.

If you write you have time to think before you commit.

If you talk there is so little time between a slip and the lip.

The writer commits to words that are firmly thought out.

The pen or keyboard allow time for review to rethink or for sorely needed correction.

Words spoken move on air waves that are transparent, elusive and fleeting.

Written words are for keeping and enduring beyond a lifetime.

Spoken words do not last but a second...no faster...they dissipate at the speed of sound.

Home video and such have not the essence of truth since they are mostly staged and don't represent much.

Selfies are silliness and trashy.

Maybe...just maybe...e-mail, twitter and the such may yet prove of enduring value.

They are stored in cyberspace for safe keeping.... maybe???

But here's a thought even a computer second guesses a delete command.

A nudge to think from a seemingly thoughtless machine.

On the other hand you can always tell someone to "shut up".

Or you can refuse to listen.

Yet, hard not to peek before a "delete" at words written.

Sometimes too much of a good thing is just too much of anything.

Too many words to say a thing is just too many words.

≈

OLD LOVE LETTERS

Try to burn an old love letter and see what happens.

As the smoke rises you once again see an entity there escaping into the vacuum of air.

Does this mixture of gases carrying a spirit presence within it?

Love letters come in many different styles and ways.

The love of a future mate.

The love of a Mother.

The pride, dignity, respect for a Father.

Brothers, Sisters and Dear Friends, these letters are all with distinctive flavors and closeness.

They are charming and light, sometimes heavy, but never, ever strange.

Not meant to be art but artistically true to being alive & affectionate.

Rich in respect and personal warmth which conveys a real, powerful feeling of heart.

A chance to read returns a heart feeling.

Love here used in the most fervent friendship and respectful meaning.

It comes from the hand of one to the eyes and heart of another.

Words so dear and true with penmanship so distinctive.

The scribe and his script of instant recognition.

Appears here again in instant deep remembrance.

≈

MANKIND NEEDS A NEW PARADIGM

A new paradigm.

A new trajectory.

Idols and paragons today are movie stars and sport stars.

These are every body's heroes.

They are imitated and emulated.

Admired and adored.

Given credit for intelligence and knowledge which they really do not possess.

They are elevated to hysterical admiration.

Admiring everything about these individuals who have major personal flaws.

Take these for example: Robin Williams, Elvis, Michael Jackson, Charlie Sheen, Lindsey Lohan.

Entertainment rather than enlightenment.

So much money thrown at one; no time for the other.

We have a brain to think.

Our most important endowment from nature.

A new paradigm for humanity.

A pursuit of personal knowledge cloaked in virtue & understanding.

≈

AWE

Like our ancestors, we bow in awe to the vastness of the heavenly sky at night and the bright sun of day.

It is awe that fuels our search for understanding and knowledge.

It is awe that is the bridge from past generations to us and on to those of the future.

It is the awe in our heart and mind which embrace the desire to learn.

Awe is our quest for knowledge.

It embraces the desire to learn, to discover, and to explain.

It is the push against what we don't know but seek to know.

It is that awe within that fuels the human knack for awareness.

We have the facility to know we are alive.

We have the talent to see beyond ourselves.

We have the flair to search the heavens.

We have the gift to understand time...that before and that to come after.

Awe is both a gift and a burden.

It is through awe that we see individual elements of nature.

We can see the mutual relationship of all elements in a way only dimly or partially perceived when knowledge was not with us.

How we handle this awe is up to each of us.

≈

VOLITION

Reason and rational are basic to survival and essential to success.

Logic is the only proper judge of values and actions.

Rationality is the basic guide to virtue.

One's fundamental values are based on reason, purpose and self-esteem.

One must live for one's own sake and not a means to the end of others.

Not sacrificing oneself to others or others to oneself.

Volition is one's action and one's spirit.

It is a consciousness and conscience

Acting in harmony with that given by nature.

It is your inner sanctum.

≈

WHY ARE WE HERE?

To most humans, this question requires a spiritual answer.

The answer lies in a religious belief.

Religion provides a final solution to all spiritual questions.

A religion and its teachings speak to the what, where, when, how and why we are here.

Torah, Bible, Koran and Scriptures provide all the knowledge necessary for spiritual truths.

A true and firm belief bolstered by deep faith calms most all troubled minds.

However for the very few, the spiritual world will continue to be a separate subject.

Answers find form to become a puzzle, a riddle, an open unanswered question.

One lifetime is never enough to provide answers and to quell such enormous doubts.

There must be a place for theology to find philosophy and vice versa.

≈

IS MODERN MAN REALLY CIVILIZED?

Our civilized life is not yet weaned of war...human propensity to create and destroy.

Slavery vestiges remain today almost 2400 years post-Plato...bias, bigotry, hatred still thrive.

Women's rights barely attended to for that same 2400+ year's post-Plato...still a way to go second class in many societies.

Man still idolizing power...human propensity to follow the leader.

Hero worship abated not at all.

Greeks were enchanted by Olympiads, Romans by gladiators, modern man by sports heroes and movie stars.

That golden age mentality of Pericles still prevails today..., to be Athenian (American) is to be superior.

Nationalism separates civilization into nations....the United Nations is a gathering of the ineptitude.

Then, there are the lawyers with all the laws that benefit they who make the laws...results in a litigation nation.

Political correctness obstructs any corrective progress that may be attempted.

Much that tells a lie about civilization.

Wars, a-bombs, terrorists,

"Allah is wakbar", "Black is beautiful".

≈

PRECIOUS NON-SCENTS

We are led through life "by-the-nose".

Nose-twitch ultimatums from parents, pastors, teachers and politicians leave us glum,

But it is our sense of smell and the odors of the world that so easily change gloom to delight.

Enchanting aromas from a begonia, an onion, and esters of every sort make us giddy.

If we but catch the waft from an oven or a bakery, we are gone.

The perfumed scents from females eclipse the common sense of most males.

Smells we love them all and their ability to foretell.

Those many tattletale scents that please our senses,

We love them,

We hate them,

They wrinkle our nose.

Those aren't pleasant,

Like that of a skunk, a sulfide, a mercaptan,

We liken to a smell from hell.

How jaded is our sense of smell?

How poorly it advises to what most hold precious?

For it is a non-odor that is the most precious to have, to love, to inhale.

It is the one we can't smell; it has no odor.

That doesn't mean it isn't ever around or that we shouldn't care.

For pure and simple it is the 'air.'

Air, that non-fragrance, our life blood needs for enriching.

One we consume but do not replenish.

Air finds unmindful passage through the nose and down the mouth,

Undetected by olfactory senses,

Finding stealth gateway to the lungs.

Air, pure non-smelling air.

The atmosphere of Earth.

An atmosphere we smell not; we see not.

It is only wind's touch that gives away air's invisibility.

Air, its meager content of oxygen we find precious.

Odorless, tasteless, invisible, its life-saving energy is in every breathe.

Leads one, yet not "by-the-nose," to wonder anew, the many things we do not appreciate.

≈

FLAVORS OF IGNORANCE

Ignorance comes in flavors.

The first flavor comes about when one ignores the use of intelligence to further life's existence.

This flavor is tasteless since it comes about when one is unwilling or unable to obtain and retain knowledge.

It is tasteless because one has not the palate to be tasteful.

The second flavor of ignorance comes about when one has both intelligence and knowledge but chooses not use them.

This flavor is bland and lacks what is known as good judgment because one is lazy.

It is bland because it contains a lot of fat and baloney.

Ignorance of the first flavor abounds on planet earth but in large part it is benign since that flavor being tasteless leaves no after taste.

Ignorance of the second kind is also rife today and it is anything but benign.

My guess is that history will show that the UN and the western world in general maintained and fed on ignorance of the second flavor.

Knowing but ignoring the ills poised by dictatorships and terrorism as evident by the bickering, dithering and delaying time and time again.

It is evident and most know, in which countries freedom, liberty and prosperity now reside.

All know where the most repression exists.

Is it any question that of the 156 countries in today's world that Libya, Iran Cuba and North Korea are at the bottom of the list?

And here at home the bickering, dithering and delaying appear time and time again.

Ignorance of the second flavor is seen in:

- the budget deficit
- fossil fuels
- social security
- health care

And what is it that is common to all instances of ignorance of the second flavor?

How can we recognize the taste of second flavor ignorance?

The flavor is distinctly one of baloney and fat called PC - Political Correctness.

When ones ears hear the term PC, one can taste and smell the baloney and fat of ignorance.

≈

THREE WISHES

In a reverie no lamp, no charm, no genie; three are granted.

Fantasy stunning cognition that three be given.

Three burst from thought to words.

Immortality.

Eternal youth.

Above average evolutionary intelligence.

So simple the wishes.

No request for riches.

Time becomes a charm.

Existing in perpetuity, a gifted youth, the bittersweet desire for insight.

Here we are.

You there, I here.

I speak, you listen.

You move, I see.

Being here.

Evolving from stromatolite and amoeba.

The offspring of bitches and bastards,

Rogues and rapists,

Puritan and sinner,

Slave and king.

Not endowed by virgin nor eunuch,

Not lesbo nor gay, who shun the past and sever the future.

Pure nature at neither best nor worst.

Pure chance that reverses entropy.

A glorious reversal of Big Bang chaos.

Immortality we have not.

Being here, a treasured prize.

Endowed by the ancestors who dodged plaque, pestilence, tragedy and war.

Pick an age, any age, any evolution, any extinction - they persevered.

Each generation two survived.

To maturity, to copulate, to continue to you and me.

We carry past time with antecedent pride.

Eternal youth we have not.

The smoothness of skin - silky and waxen,

The blush of cheek - rosy and fresh;

Molts to the red of eye, sag of skin and flab of groin.

Wish not for freshness but cherish the fortune.

Take the many sunrises given after youth has passed.

Intelligence is to the mind so kind.

So fortunate to be normal.

Wisdom comes with age if one is not lazy.

Acceptance of limitations, limits life but hinders not the dance.

Thoughts proceed; below the peaks between the troughs.

The chance to sing with ideas and listen to the echo resound.

Take from the ancestors to pass forward with the originality of a personal degree.

It is all a charm.

Self-awareness.

Consciousness.

And above all the most evolutionary of gifts, a conscience.

The past is ours - me and they.

The present is mine - me alone.

The future is not for me but seed and ovum.

≈

RETIRED AND THE AMERICAN CHARACTER

Many of us are retired.

We are jobless and out to pasture.

In a way, maybe a minor way and maybe much more, it can be a national and personal crisis.

A crisis because work was more than earning a living, it was a spiritual event.

That long career gave more than money, it gave an identity.

It wasn't only a paycheck, it was so much more.

When we worked we took part in the daily life of humanity.

Work gave each of us both a purpose and stability.

It provided a means to integrate with others and share a mission.

But when we retired, all that was before, changed.

It's a kind of a catastrophe, not necessarily to the individual, but to humanity.

All that experience, knowledge and skills learned through success and failure is now set aside.

Retirees are still alive and happy to think.

They collectively hold huge amounts of American genius

Genius that now sits idle in garages, or in an attic, or sitting on a back porch.

Most often retirees still want to speak and desire to share all that they have learned.

They have so much that is good and rich in character.

They have achieved what all seek to be...healthy, wealthy, and wise.

Even though many retirees find hobbies or charities or small businesses so much real experience and wisdom becomes unused.

It is obvious that often 30 or more years of our life is spent in retirement.

Might this be poor use of a public wealth dividend?
Might this be ignoble and selfish action on the retiree's part?

Should older adults be expected to play a legacy role of lasting value?

Might American life need a new paradigm?

Should universities or business create a repository of expertise available on call?

Or some concept similar to the Peace Core which use retirees to bolster capitalism?

Just might a matrix be created which pair bonds retirees and novices to lessen learning curves?

There lies in the retired a huge gold mine (mind) and a mother lode of experience waiting to be exploited by some enterprising capitalist.

Could the retired be missing a good bet for leaving lasting legacies?

What about an AARP with real purpose, a lasting essence, and true value? Is it in the cards?

≈

IN DEFENSE OF MARRIAGE

It's raining, the wind is blowing hard.

The trees are whipping around every which way with tornadic vengeance only nature can create.

Nature today is showing its ass.

So I sit with pen in hand and begin to think about "gay marriage."

Something today that has become a buzz word and another reason for some to cry.

I know nature holds no contempt for human life - hell she created it.

Yet I wonder does humankind hold contempt for nature.

Humans somehow, someway need to believe in naturalness of things.

Believe in the reality of the universe of nature and all that is.

There is a star called "Sun" which shines so elegantly on our home - Planet Earth.

Earth is that glorious and elegant place of dirt and water that is our only home.

Earth is the unique and primordial source of life - or so we believe.

It is where we humans have become the pinnacle of intelligence.

Life proliferated in crucial stages to get to where we are now.

One such stage was some 540 million years ago when life found its eucaryotic nature.

Eucaryotic, a big word, which means true kernel or nucleus.

It's when the nature of egg and sperm became natural.

It's what we humans now call sex.

It's what makes life's greatest division - male and female.

It's what makes life more than remaining mere sexless bacteria.

We of humankind learned fire and developed language.

Through observation and with the intelligence and sexual reproduction we have excelled.

How consistent, how best, can we of humankind stay in line with nature.

So the question:

"If Male/Female relationship is normal, is in line, is consistent, is harmonious with nature and...

Humankind now defines this truth of nature as the institution of marriage as a correct definition of this natural truth

Why then is humankind considering uni-species as an alternate consideration for marriage.

Nature in its ever-advancing search for higher intelligence and greater awareness abandoned bacterium as of any true destiny eons ago.

On what basis is humankind adopting a reversal of a natural law?

Does "political correctness" trump nature?

Has humankind found its newest and latest Tower of Babel?

Or might we maintain marriage in its prime directive to legitimize and maximize the continuing of the species.

It is the natural way to advance, evolve, and become better than we are now.

It is nature's way that knows in order to reproduce, to thrive, to progress then a normal man-woman relationship is required.

Nature knows full well it dies in a single generation with the abnormal.

That is a natural truth to itself.

And besides are no traditions sacred?

≈

IN DEFENSE OF GENTLEMEN

Men who harass or assault women are not gentlemen.

Most often they are self-serving egotists.

They have two ugly personality traits which they amplify with power.

Aggressive masculinity ...they find power over women a sexual turn-on.

Loveless sexuality ...they prefer sex without intimacy.

They seek promiscuous sex or multiple partners.

Then sport the conquests, like notches on a gun.

These predators tend to have sexist attitudes.

Opposition to gender equality their hidden mantra.

A traditional role for women their concealed goal.

Seize them by the hair and drag.

They are slobs who are lecherous, greedy and manipulative.

They use and abuse women like a licentious, lascivious wolf.

Presidential power enough to besmirch a naïve lass by soiling her blue dress.

Always adding to their power with a smirch and a swagger.

Not all men should be tagged with the mark of the beast.

It's only a certain type of man who uses power in predatory ways.

A real man is courteous and honorable.

Gentle first, if not chivalrous.

He proceeds with understanding.

Self-control is his main stay.

It's not what he wears or drives.

It's how he behaves, who he is.

He has both manners and morals.

Uses politeness when situations are trying.

He has his own dignity and shows respect.

He's not pushy, manipulative or belittling.

He seeks friendship not ownership.

Encourages a woman to be a woman.

Sometimes it's hard to be a gentleman.

For fewer women seem interested in being ladies.

Women have lost track.

In their exuberance for equality they shun modesty.

Women have thrown femininity aside.

Aside, when they idolize and imitate females who dress skanky.

Many now talk and act crudely.

Expect respect but trashing any way but their way in a "how dare you attitude."

Split the dress down to the navel, up to the thigh,

A see-through leaving little to the imagination,

And then invoking indignation for the stare.

Taking the moral high ground in all instances.

Yet demanding the freedom to choose while belittling those who cherish a fetus.

Might the solution be?

Men be gentle. Women be ladies.

≈

RED LIGHTS & PORNOGRAPHY & SEXUAL CONFLICTS

A visit to Amsterdam.

Of course, a walk through the red-light district.

A red-light district must be the oldest shopping mall in the world.

Women have all the shops; men do all the shopping.

I do believe it to be a bit strange that most women do not regard prostitutes as low life.

But they do condemn men for the shopping experience.

Despite who pays and who gains.

To be candid, I do think some women may actually envy the capitalistic traits of those sales ladies.

They make use of a natural endowment and profit from its sale.

They have a lock on the entire market.

Its renewable.

Talk about a non-competitive edge.

Ladies like Delilah, Diamond Lil, Mata Hari, and Stormy Daniels.

They bring to heel men of the powerful and the mighty.

Without much doubt prostitutes and painted ladies are both victim and accomplices to the sins of lust.

Anyhow, I got to further thinking about the many and often used comparison of sexes.

Now it is not my intent to offend any senses.

Nor to debate this issue or raise your ire.

But some of the comparisons I can think of are a bit coarse.

So take this in good humor and with a grain of salt...

shot of booze or whatever.

I began to list the many ways that men and women approach things differently.

More specifically how they often treat sex, red lights and pornography in tell-tale ways.

A takeoff on the theme that men are from Mars; women from Venice.

Remember only meant to make you smile on how we fool each other.

What I jokingly state below, just voices modern day sexual norms.

Male - I just want to have sex.

Female -I need a commitment.

Male - It's only certain parts of your body that I'm interested in.

Female - It's all of me or nothing.

Female - I can show as much cleavage as I want.

Don't let me catch you peeking.

And you're a pervert if you stare.

Male - The same God that gave you those boobies gave me these eyes.

Man - Nice cleavage.

Woman - I see what you're staring at stupid.

Woman - Confessing first time was in a back seat.

Man - Wondering if it was a Ford or Chevy.

Woman - I know exactly what you're thinking.

Man - I'm glad you do, right now, I don't have a lick of sense.

Men - Want women they never had.

Women - Date preparation includes a shack-up sack.

Men - Brag about notches on their gun.

Women - Smile thinking about the men they satisfied.

Men - Proud of the women they bedded down.

Women - Delighted with the men they put to slumber.

Man - I'm done its time to sleep.

Woman - I'm wide awake it's time to think.

Man - Was that good for you.

Women - Oh yes (out loud). No, you didn't find the right spot dumb ass (to self).

Women - Not tonight, it's my time of the month.

Man - I'll do the wash by hand.

Man - Embarrassed by the premature ejaculation.

Woman - Got you, with a smile of I win again.

Woman - No. No. I never do myself.

Man - Yeah, I use toys too.

Man - I'm done.

Woman - Didn't know you started.

Man – You're the best I ever had.

Woman- Well that's nice. I'm still looking.

Man - Rolling off.

Woman - Wish he'd take the wet spot with him.

Man – Let's do this again sometime.

Woman - Sorry, I never make the same mistake twice.

Man - Snoring.

Woman - Staring at the ceiling.

Man - How do I leave quietly?

Woman - Wish he gets the hell out of here; I need to get some sleep.

Man - What was I thinking, I must have been drunk.

Woman - Don't have to wait until morning, I already hate myself.

Man - I ain't ever gonna do this ugly bitch again.

Woman - This low life slob ain't never gonna do me again.

Man - I'm sorry if I knew you were a virgin, I would have taken my time.

Woman - If I knew you had time, I would have taken off my panty hose.

Man - As she wraps her legs around him, he says I didn't know you were so passionate.

Woman - I'm not! I'm painting my toenails.

Man - God approves of oral sex. He made it look like a taco.

Woman - Smiling. (no comment)

Man - God made little boys of string. He had a little left over so he left me a thing.

Woman - God made little girls of lace. He didn't have enough so I now have a space.

Man - Here try on my pants.

Woman - Why would I do that.

Man - Just see how they fit.

Woman - Wow these are way too big for me.

Man - And you remember that.

Woman - Here, try on my panties

Man - Gets them only up to his knees and says I can't get into these.

Woman - And you never will until you change your attitude

All of the above is written in jest!

But what about when both get it right.

When the male and the female find an attachment.

Not when sex is the final end but sex becomes what satisfies a longing for a complete attachment to another human being.

One not only emotional but physical like when two bolts of radiance converge to strike the same magical hidden spots.

Where a torrent of self-abandonment and amorous desires become an immediate desire to unite in the most natural way.

When passion overwhelms, and all other senses depart but for the uniting of protrusion and inclusion requires a seal of extasy delight.

When time matters not and desire for the other consumes all else.

Where penetration and acceptance matches acceptance and deliverance.

When now no longer can be postponed and union must be consumed.

Deliverance and acceptance seals the act.

The first insertion again renewing a virgin trust.

Across the sensitive clitoris mound and a parting of the vaginal ring.

The folding back of hymen tissue matching foreskin reverse slide

Penetration accepted with female loins raised forward lifting trust accepting fully the push of insertion.

The desire to accept his full protrusion.

Both willingly accepting the desire to fulfill and enshrine that which is entering a hidden domain.

Man - WOW!

Woman - WOW! WOW!!!

≈

PADDLING

To spank or not to spank that is the question.

The answer is don't sweat the small stuff.

And spanking is small stuff.

The question better to address is how to define parental duties.

Answer: There are no greater absolutes to life and the human race than parenting.

Parenting duties are teaching discipline, morality and the truth about how the world works.

Parents must encourage imagination; explain the art of conversation and the joy of thinking.

Parents need to remember that the world is composed of peer pressure and sometimes bullying.

It does not take a village to raise children; it takes proper parenting.

Surely tactics to parenting includes whether to spank or not.

Nature seems to dictate that boys need a good whack now and then, but girls less so.

Nature also shows, that in general by the age of five spanking is of little value.

Maybe a 2x4 is then best used; but by fourteen only the wood gets broken.

What are some signs of poor parenting?

Well for females its "mother stupid."

For the male it's being a "dead-beat dad."

Women generally are excellent mothers.

Their shortcoming is they never let go.

Mothers are bent on protecting forever even when inappropriate.

Under the premise of not turn a back they will protect a wayward offspring.

For males the worst parenting sin is being a deadbeat.

A proper dad will provide for children dutifully with responsibility and consistency without being asked.

Good parenting means doing the right thing when right is in conflict with love.

It means doing right regardless of the consequences to a loved one.

It means doing the right thing even if the loved one feels abandoned or betrayed.

It's called hard love and is the age-old story line, second only in conflict between good and evil.

Hard love is a real and common human trauma, one which every one of us has experienced at one time or another.

Unfortunately, often one does not use hard love but instead follows the easy route of supporting a love one based on unconditional love.

Choosing love over right is equal to not doing the right thing.

The reality of it all is that none of us get smart on parenting until the child is grown.

Which then begs another question - "Do children raise parents."

≈

MODERN DAY POLITICS

The pendulum swings much too violent.
No sine-wave discipline to the movement.
Hanging to; pausing fro; seldom balance in the center.

Too many claims of main spring importance.
Gears and teeth, mouths and speech, seek no mesh.
Coils deliberately sprung meant to impede.

Might the problem be.
Disturb the tempo.
Intentionally affect the movement.
Clog ideals with an ego.
Disturb the action.
Over wind.
Tamper with pendulum swing.

Confuse those whose time is precious.
Forget that good times need balance.
Be not open to repair.

Delay and stall.
Cause despair.

Not important for stable time to share.

≈

THE LOST GOLDEN OPPORTUNITY

The baton of greatness is handed to few.

They need grasp it tightly, sprint forward and run.

Mind and spirit concentrated on the lane ahead.

Seldom does historic time open itself to greatness.

The right individual to see the vision and grab destiny's baton.

Elected President creates a sprinting aspiration to shape the human race.

The first black president's golden opportunity.

He was the ideal man to un-hyphenate the country.

Simple statements from a voice of vision makes for difference.

The race to make the dreams of King its trophy.

A lane of Jeffersonian individuality and Lincoln equality.

Amalgamating gold into America's melting pot of people.

An open opportunity to America's long slow pace of progressive fusion.

A kick-start ahead when unity of race, ethnicity and color becomes the guiding light.

Had the sprinter concentrated on getting the hyphen out.

The lamp of destiny was never lit.

A race to amalgamate received no power.

The hyphen of separation covert or invert accentuated and emphasized.

He of mixed race shunned heritage.

The Mother Caucasian – the Father African.

Had "Dreams from My Father" but was raised by another.

He grasped not the baton of Martin nor shared his dream.

Sought not to run in the lane of the good fellow King.

In the song of Chuck Berry "Ain't that a shame".

A MODEST VOTING PROPOSAL

A voter must determine his or her personal values.

These values should be clearly defined to self.

Candidates must then be selected against the voter's values.

Take, for instance, the next election.

My basic values of government are twofold.

- Keep me safe.
- Maintain rule of law.

My secondary consideration, although not lesser requirements, are:

- Smaller government.

- Lower taxes.
- More liberty.

With your selected criteria one should vote and opt for worthy candidates.

Based solely on personal values and not derogatory media ads and superficial claims and assertions.

≈

FAITH

Faith is a human passion lacking logic.

An act of trust requiring no substantiation.

Often running in the face of countervailing evidence.

Using stories and fables of questionable authenticity.

Yet faith puts things in order.

Gives a certainty to life that all seek and crave.

Copes well with feelings of inadequacy.

Invokes humility to answer the profound.

Must be human to seek it.

Easy to find; hard to lose.

A galvanizing force granting a meaning to life.

Creates design for existence.

Faith is mental suicide.

Fits neatly into a belief folder.

The one labeled fear factor relief.

Relief from the unknown and the unknowable.

≈

SEARCH

Faith is a world-wide phenomenon.

It has a deep presence in the human psychic.

Possibly too much does it persist, endure and power over human beings.

The fear is that mankind and its current form of civilization may doom itself.

Much too many lead their lives based on faith alone.

Faith becomes the sole reason for human existence.

In any event deep faith and true belief is a human reality.

One that cannot be ignored.

To do anything else is to ignore humanity for what it is now.

For mankind to reach a meaningful civilization, what is needed are three important aims.

Namely:

- One language for unambiguous communication.

- One race for color-blindness.
- One belief to unite with purpose.

Now the first two goals are attainable.

There is good progress being made.

It is the third which is the real issue.

Let all individuals keep their chosen belief.

Each individual must show gratitude and appreciation for this one chance at existence.

Each must acknowledge a desire to live to its fullest regardless of birth assets and deficits.

We seem to be aware that there is something more to life than we realize.

What that is we do not honestly know.

So we have faith to ease an unknowing.

Is that something so obvious that it shouldn't be dismissed.

Is it a desire, a goal, to centralize the human mind?

One that extends beyond the conscious, beyond the imagination, beyond what we call a soul?

Might there be a something within the intelligence and ingenuity possessed by the average man.

A destiny which inspires the advance of man.

One which might recognize a material and unconventional destiny.

In any event I must say I just don't know.

I really and truly don't rightly know.

So in place of faith I employ search.

What I find, if I find, is my life's endeavor.

≈

FAITH AND UNDERSTANDING

There is so much in what the good book proclaims.

Adds serenity and ease to the quality of life.

Requires one to be patient, humble and meek.

That which some of us possess so little of.

All which the bible says is so true.

But one still wonders who are the humans to be trusted?

Who are we to listen to?

Ourselves? Others?

If both then to what degree each?

And how to separate truth from fiction?

Rely on faith! I think not!

It puts too much reliance on the judgment, opinions and direction that others define.

That is a rub.

Love! ... A human passion.

Wonderful to itself.

Albeit much too whimsical.

Trust! … By definition is to believe in something.

Thus to have faith by trusting becomes a circular argument.

Hope! ... Is to wish.

To allow the vagrancies of life a role.

Best saved for Las Vegas.

Yet faith puts things in order.

Gives a certainty to life that all seek and crave.

Copes well with feelings of inadequacy.

Invokes humility to answer the profound.

Must be human to seek it.

Easy to find; hard to lose.

Faith cannot be viewed as a mental shortcoming.

It has much too deep a presence in the human psychic to be dismissed.

What is of concern is the reality of its persistence, endurance and power over human beings.

My fear is that mankind and its current form of civilization may doom itself by faith alone.

Much too many lead their lives based on faith alone.

Faith becomes the sole reason for human existence.

In any event deep faith and true belief is a human reality.

One that cannot be ignored; should not be ignored.

To do anything else is to ignore humanity for what it is now.

For mankind to reach for a meaningful civilization what is needed are three important goals to be met.

Namely:

- One language for unambiguous communication.
- One race for color-blindness.
- One belief to unite with purpose.

Now the first two goals are attainable.

There is good progress being made.

It is the third which is the real problem.

Let all individuals keep their chosen belief.

Each individual must show gratitude and appreciation for this one chance at existence.

Each must acknowledge a desire to live to its fullest regardless of birth assets and deficits.

We seem to be aware that there is something more to life than we realize.

What that is I do not know.

Is it something so obvious that it shouldn't be dismissed?

Is it a desire, a goal, to centralize the human mind?

One that extends beyond the conscious, beyond the imagination.

Yet within the intelligence and ingenuity possessed by the average man.

A destiny which inspires the advance of man.

One which recognizes a material and unconventional destiny.

In any event I must say I just don't know.

I really and truly don't rightly know.

So in place of faith I employ search.

What I find, if I find, is my life's endeavor.

Now an introspective rub!

In all I write here, there is a disconnect.

Worldwide ninety-five percent of people have deep faith.

Faith is similar to love and /or trust, they are all human passions.

Faith lacks logic but gives a rich tapestry to our lives.

It adds more than certainty to life that has little to do with fables, questionable or otherwise.

Without faith, love and trust, what is left to give purpose to our lives?

One might add hope to this group as well.

Having lived life as long as I have, I might say with a straight face that any of this fits into a folder?

Life is part of the wind that swirls us around and takes us to our destinies.

We begin to believe we control that which has been predestined for us.

Though destiny is preordained, we think we have the power to choose which way to swing our lives.

Alas, faith then comes into play - faith that we make the right choice to enrich our life span on earth.

Trusting there be a heaven.

"Faith and Understanding" is not meant to be an essay.

Merely the projection of a series of thoughts.

No ego involved; no sermon intended.

No lesson, but surely debatable.

≈

HATRED

I'm on a hunt for some psychological answers.

I'm wondering why and when humans developed hatred.

How did it come to be?

Did it originate as a foil to fear or is it revenge based?

I'm doing my own research on the subject.

But I really would like a faith-based opinion on it and look for a true understanding or a religious explanation.

I have been reading on human emotions and feelings and the one that intrigues me is hatred.

Most others I can understand from my own base but not so with hatred.

A dislike I can judge is based on the senses; but hatred is a feeling buried inside which comes from I know not what.

What might a preacher think about hatred?

It seems to me that most religions have a hard time culling this feeling from their brethren.

Yet hatred is the antithesis of brotherly love, so both can't possibly reside in a true religion nor in an ethical individual.

Hatred is ground so deep in many humans as to be in-extractable.

Much of today's world problems stem from hatred.

Hatred is one if not the most vile of feeling that an individual could possess.

Ignore this if you like but I'll still be on the prowl.

THE DEVIL WITHIN

The devil within us and not the devil outside.

Now that's something to really spend some time analyzing.

The devil originated from angel pride - not a good belief.

The devil is human.

God didn't create the devil........we did.

In biblical terms - we still, today, are taking bites out of that apple;

some small bites others the whole damn apple.

Hatred originated within us - not a good enough explanation for the excessive hatred in the world.

No doubt hatred exists in each of us to a greater or lesser degree.

But where and how does it come to be in us, and why excess in some?

The devil that lives in one's soul- is the source of hate.

But it can't be original sin; babies are too innocent to sin or hate.

No doubt he lies within but how did he get in?

And why does he grow out of control in some?

We were all born pure with a pure soul, a pure conscience.

What mucked that up?

Certainly not the God within us.

The devil within us?

Maybe but where did he come from and how did he get in?

Let's dwell on this for a while.

IMPRINTED

In deserts - the lands of sand.

Where so many others questioned the gods.

Answers received always require a return to earth.

Are we predestined or do we have free will?

Are genes given at birth tattooed with indelible ink?

Are the latitudes and longitudes of life set within a narrow degree?

Does one no longer reach to the heavens?

Now one finds the answers in cyberspace and not with the God.

≈

AN ARABIAN AFFAIR

A SAUDI CANDLE & THE AMERICAN MATCH

The candle, tapered tallow, a white cotton wick, tasseled and shallow.

Casual to any reason that there be a need to glow.

Unaware that to shine it requires a flame from another.

How sensational the strike of a match.

The ignition, a spark, the white-hot flash.

Friction the key, the start of the burn.

Smells of brimstone and sulfur awash in the air.

The energy of the match across a global expanse sets the stage and offers a mutual magnificent affair.

The tallow was dormant, unaware of potential, a virgin

inexperienced in the technology of the other.

The match with its offer - a crude proposal; the candle open to enticement but its desires satisfied only if gold.

Dynamic the match with the heat from a strike seeks further potential from within the tallow of the candle.

Linked together in an intimate concession, the flame of a match endears itself to the white wick of the candle.

Hot is the match, awash with the heat of discovery unable to squelch its zeal for the candles potential.

The match is energetic with high hopes for the other, the candle unsure of itself slow to be lit.

The reluctant candle held back by nomadic tradition, ever so slow to catch up to the hot-head match.

For the candle to begin an ignite, the match must kindle, coax and gently tutor into an initial delight.

The match knows that once the candle is lit, it will be surely necessary to find the right fit.

While the match continues to blaze, it's head now a char, its body still on fire setting the pace.

Not a pause to its unrefined desires, the match yields its entire body to that which it desires.

The candle with its lazy wick, a simple past, steeped in tradition would rather let today, idle away, and not go too fast.

Knowing not the potential the match breeds, the candle has no need to aspire, why need that which was not needed before.

The match continues its fiery burn, the light of its passion needing to kindle the slow hesitant candle to turn.

Finally and slowly the candle shows a faint spark, no longer able to resist the heat of the match, it flickers and ever so slowly begins to awake.

It sparks, it falters, it rises, it falls, it is so slow to purposeful ignition.

By now the match has burnt beyond its own charred tip.

Never known to falter; not ever to give up.

It further offers the potential of its stout stick.

Knowing itself once started, not able to stop its own uncontrollable appetite for fulfillment.

Must transfer all of its passion to the lethargic latent candle that is still reluctant to rely on its own.

The hotter the blaze; the shorter the duration.

The match gradually starts to expire.

While the candle manages to steady its own glow.

Seeking the energy in itself to form a transition.

Searching for the confidence that within itself it can endure and inspire.

With ample time and assistance, the candle finds its pace.

Having weaned its way from the flame of its birth.

It has become no longer needy and began in itself to believe.

The match moves on its way to expire, burnt away, no longer a need.

Orange embers along full length showing a dying existence.

With some feeble wisp of smoke, faint heat rises from the spent match.

With its dying embers, it knows it can't last.

Falling to the side, it now lay prone.

Cold and dead black, a crumpled-up snake of spent ash.

Bent and fractured, black sooty remains, its body it used as its own pyre.

Self-immolated by setting itself on fire.

It has become a corpse, now shriveled, a mummy of dust.

No hint, no memory, no token, no gravestone for a marker.

Merely a shell of ash of forgotten achievement and trust.

Without hesitation, the candle's flame continues to burn.

Believing in it to be able and fit.

Generating energy and wealth for a time yet measured.

The wonder is whether in a quiet moment of introspection.

Might the candle have formed tears of separation.

Like waxen tears dripping down passing over a cheek.

Will it acknowledge the match now charred and forgotten.

With its hot burning wick, the melted tallow finds passage over the edge.

Cascading slowly along the sides.

Do the long strings of tallow create torrent of remorse?

Solidifying into mounds of regret pooling at the feet.

Or might it be?

As the unchecked tallow melts, so much excess carelessly falls to the sides.

Swelled with position, a backsliding to tradition.

Pools of spent drippings form solids of waste.

Mounds of which form at the base.

Certainly, indeed, the candle has no need to recognize what kindled its existence.

Things came too easy; it all lay below ground where the candle maker herded his sheep.

It was all God-given - the tallow, the spark.

No need to put forth appreciation or recognition.

It was something deserved by its own isolated position.

≈

THE AMERICAN TRAPPER

"A Legacy Ignored".

"A Legacy Abused",

"A Legacy Slandered".

Let us first remind ourselves that the richness of this country is not just its natural resources, be that plentiful, but it is of equal importance to recognize the great men who took those first steps forward to open this great land.

The first of the first were trappers. They were the first to walk the cold north eastern complexes of the Delaware, the Hudson, the Susquehanna and the Adirondacks, where mink and muskrat populated the lakes and rivers. The trappers moved unto the southern lands of the Blue Ridge, The Smokey's, The Appalachians, where the otter, the beaver, the bear and winged creatures lived. They were the first to cross the heartland and raft the Ohio and the magnificent Mississippi. They girded the Great Lakes and looked eagerly to the western slopes while they canoed the endless Missouri and its tributaries.

Trappers were the first non-native Americans with the right stuff, but they were of a different breed, yet still of our American breed. Different enough that mainstream America views them now with myopic and jaundice eyes. It has become:

"A Legacy Ignored".

It was not the cowboy, the rancher, the cavalry, the settlers, or the railroaders that first opened the West. They all came later - much later. Hark back when it was the Native Americans who populated the land, No criticism -intended but the Indian Tribes throughout America were still in the Stone Age with no metals, no written language, no alphabet and only a very rich verbal history. English, French, Dutch and Spanish settlers may have colonized the East but pioneering west of the Mississippi belonged to the American trapper. The first boots to cross a moccasin trail was that of a trapper, If the real picture of time could be painted, one would have to show the trapper as one with the Indian and with Nature. The trapper emulated the Indian's ways, their dress, and their techniques. The trapper was that unique transition and preservative between the natural and the modern. The American trapper had no intention of owning or taking land. The trapper just like the Indian never thought he needed or was entitled to owning land. It belonged to nature. It allowed man and animal the means to survive. True American man whether he is trapper or Indian was in a harmonious and synergistic state that animal rights activists could never know nor understand. And yet even worse -not want to understand. It is

"A Legacy Abused".

The trapper by-and-large admired and emulated the Indian. But alas, the Indian's heritage is but a shadow of its former self. They now live on reservations, or granted land and are trying so hard to maintain their heritage. Their way of life is gone. They hang on with pride alone or with a Casino. Most probable the most satisfied Indian today is one who is also a trapper. A strange reversal isn't it! But I don't want to dwell on the Indian that is another story. I want to honor the American trapper for what he did and what he is today.

The trapper today is not very different than those of yesteryear. In fact it amazes me how little the individual trapper has changed. They are much the same type of independent and unique men and women (yes women) with the same core values. They desire nothing other.than to-be one with nature .They are- above all true conservationists. Despite this trueness to nature they are an endangered species. They are condemned and slandered by the animal rights activists and are thought of poorly by the General Public.

They have:"A Legacy Slandered."

Why is this? Trappers have evolved and endured as have most Americans when it comes to the environment, conservation, and maintenance of all species. But trappers are actually more in tuned than most because they live closer to nature. They spend more time and set more footprints in the great outdoors in one year than do most folk in a lifetime.

What Americans in general do not know is that the great trapper's spirit lives yet today in the hearts and souls of a select few? Trappers are a solitary and quiet lot. It is not so strange therefore, that they are forgotten by most. They do not trumpet themselves, their ways, and what they do. All Americans today, need to remember that the footprint of our great country was first imprinted by the trapper. Americans in general thinks highly of Davy Crocket, Daniel Boone, Lewis and Clark. The spirit of these great men still exists in a small group of humble Americans. Americans in general may not know these individuals by name but we do know them as trappers. They have tradition with them. They are America's first tradition.

I've been following a small group of these trappers in Texas and I can say they are humble people with a great spirit. They pride themselves with trapper individuality. They have tradition within them. They wear their individual personalities on their sleeves or in their long hair and bent hats or in a tooth necklace. They have kept an American legacy alive. These Trappers, they don't want much and ask for nothing. They wish to pursue their own unique way of life. They just want to have their own little section of the American way. They do a lot of natural conservation, a lot of just plain woodsy folk lore, a little bit of good and very little harm. Who of us can say as much?

Trapping is an American way of life - a legacy - a heritage. Unlike any other part of the world, America is different. Asia, Africa and Europe were populated by some ancient migration of people over thousands if not tens of thousands of years. America was opened in mere decades by men of character, men of boldness, men of self-reliance. Men who above everything else loved the solidarity with nature and loved the lure of the land. These often solitary individuals did not destroy or abuse Nature. Each felt they were but a mere speck in a vast wilderness. Each was, as is the trapper of today, a minority in the vast population. A minority, very rich in legacy and heritage. They are a legacy, a heritage, a breed apart which the general public either doesn't know or thinks of poorly of them. The animal rights activists vow to exterminate them. It is not the animals of our land that are being pushed to extinction, it is the trapper who is endangered. The animal rights activists seek to crush a legacy.

Let us talk and compare a little between the trapper and the animal rights activist. An animal rights activist and most nearly all of the general public know what a fox looks like. But the trapper knows:

the fox and he knows what the fox knows. The trapper can detail a fox's habits, haunts, foods, instincts, his very essence, his captive being. The animal rights activist and the public hears and reads about a fox's slyness, The trapper knows first-hand the cunningness of a fox and he will give you numerous examples of the abilities of the many foxes he has personally known. The trapper not only knows the fox and his traits, he admires the creature for every one of his abilities. Can the animal rights activist say the same? The trapper knows intimately the coyote; the badger, the wolf the mountain lion The animal rights activist may know what a coyote howl sounds like, but the trapper can tell the call of a male, a female, the yip of the young and they can tell you what the call means. Trappers know and respect animals for exactly what they are - wild creatures true to their own nature.

The trapper is indeed a minority - a very small minority. For example, maybe five hundred in the whole great state of Texas. The general public opinion is at best neutral and uninterested in the trappers life and ways. Why should Texans pay any attention to a breed of five hundred? The country in general, pays little attention to the trapper and so be it. But the animal rights activists who are also a small but vocal minority have self-ordained themselves to speak for all. They use what they perceive as morals to foster their contrary to nature cause. They intend to herd the general public to their position by any means. The real rules of nature become secondary to their own arbitrary rulings.

Animal Rights Activist ignores the legacy.

Animal Rights Activists abuse the legacy

Animal Rights Activists slander the legacy

The Trapper may no longer be the premier pioneer of old and maybe he is not one-with the Indian any longer. But even today he is one with nature and a true conservationist to the Earth in a way unequaled and often misunderstood by most.

Let's let today's trapper be an American Legacy and continue that unique and synergistic transition between the natural and the modern.

The Trapper asks only that all Americans let them preserve and keep alive the Legacy - Their way of life.

About the Author

DON ERDEK

Don was born on December 21, 1935, in Manville, a small New Jersey factory town where he spent his early childhood. He graduated with high honors from Rutgers University in 1963 earning a degree in chemistry. He took a position with prestigious Bell Labs in Murray Hill, New Jersey and continued his education with a graduate study program in chemical physics at the Brooklyn Institute of Technology. He moved to Miami, Florida in 1965 and shortly thereafter took a job on Eniwetok Atoll in the South Pacific followed by one in Tripoli Libya, then one in Saudi Arabia that lasted some eighteen years more. He retired in May 1991 at the age of fifty-six. He was lured out of retirement to take a position with Johnson Controls at Cape Canaveral. Working at the Cape on the space program and specifically on the launch towers was an exciting challenge. He retired once again in 1996 and purchased a seventy-three-acre ranch in Colmesneil, Texas in the deep East Texas piney woods. Was a rancher for seventeen years on one of the most beautiful pieces of God's green Earth. Moved to Naples, Florida in 2015.

He decided it was time to write a book with a poetic take on life, which led to his first book "Inner Sanctum. Don found he still had many stories and poems he wanted to share so he collected them into this book, "The Ochre Hand".

This is his legacy, his final sharing of his wit, wisdom and ever searching for answers. Don left us the evening of August 16, 2020 just as this book was being published.

www.ingramcontent.com/pod-product-compliance
Lightning Source LLC
Chambersburg PA
CBHW021103110726
47900CB00007B/2003

* 9 7 8 0 5 7 8 2 3 5 8 7 5 *